四川好女人

The Good Woman of Setzuan

Bertolt Brecht ◆ 著

劉森堯 ◆ 譯

The Good Woman of Setzuan

四川好女人

Bertolt Brecht ◆ 著　劉森堯 ◆ 譯

國家圖書館出版品預行編目 (CIP) 資料

四川好女人 / Bertolt Brecht 著 ; 劉森堯譯.
-- 二版. -- 臺北市 : 書林, 2020.08
面 ;　公分. -- (愛看戲 ; 8)
譯自 : The good woman of Setzuan
ISBN 978-957-445-890-5(平裝)

875.55　　　　109009574

愛看戲❽

四川好女人 第二版

The Good Woman of Setzuan

著　　者	Bertolt Brecht
譯　　者	劉森堯
執行編輯	周佩蓉
校　　對	王建文
出 版 者	書林出版有限公司 100 台北市羅斯福路四段 60 號 3 樓 Tel (02) 2368-4938 · 2365-8617 Fax (02) 2368-8929 · 2363-6630
台北書林書店	106 台北市新生南路三段 88 號 2 樓之 5 Tel (02) 2365-8617
學校業務部	Tel (02) 2368-7226 · (04) 2376-3799 · (07) 229-0300
經銷業務部	Tel (02) 2368-4938
發 行 人	蘇正隆
郵　　撥	15743873 · 書林出版有限公司
網　　址	http://www.bookman.com.tw
經銷代理	紅螞蟻圖書有限公司 台北市內湖區舊宗路二段 121 巷 19 號 Tel (02) 2795-3656(代表號) Fax (02) 2795-4100
登 記 證	局版臺業字第一八三一號
出版日期	2006 年 8 月一版，2020 年 8 月二版初刷
定　　價	260 元
I S B N	978-957-445-890-5

目次

THE GOOD WOMAN OF SETZUAN

布萊希特小傳

布萊希特 (Bertolt Brecht, 1898-1956) 於一八九八年二月十日出生在德國巴伐利亞地區的奧格斯堡 (Augsburg)，父親是工廠的經理。他從年輕時代開始就產生激進的思想，在柏林和慕尼黑大學時，起先主修自然科學和醫學，但他的主要興趣還是在文學和戲劇上面。大學畢業後從事劇場工作，二〇年代中在柏林的劇場發展出他有名的「史詩劇場」理論，以「疏離原則」為出發點，主張觀眾看戲時應保持距離，不應投入情感，舞台力求簡化，引用敘述者，使用默劇動作、歌唱及幻燈片等，藉此減少觀眾情感投入的機會，以擴展觀眾思考反省的空間。「史詩劇場」的理論和實務於五〇年代及布萊希特死後的六〇年代，曾經在西方劇場上喧騰一時。布萊希特於一九二八年以《三便士歌劇》(*Three Penny Opera*) 一劇聲名大噪。三〇年代中，希特勒掌權之後，他被迫流亡法國、瑞典、蘇聯及美國等地，居無定所。他的幾齣著名作品如《勇氣媽媽》(*Mother Courage and Her Children*, 1939)、《伽利略》(*Galileo*, 1939) 及《四川好女人》(*The Good Woman of Setzuan*, 1940) 等都是在流亡期間所寫就，他的最後一齣重要作品《高加索灰闌記》(*The Caucasian Chalk Circle*) 寫於一九四五年。第二次世界大戰之後，他返回德國，定居東柏林，組織著名的「總體劇團」，他同時是個激進的馬克斯主義者，他死於一九五六年，享年五十八歲。

譯序

《四川好女人》與「史詩劇場」

希萊希特於一九五六年去世，他畢生提倡不遺餘力的「史詩劇場」在他死後不久即在大西洋兩岸的歐美各地風行起來，特別是他死前兩年的一九五四年，柏林的「總體劇團」應邀在巴黎演出《勇氣媽媽》一劇，得到空前的成功而獲得極熱烈的響應，「史詩劇場」的理論和實踐遂逐漸風行開來，如果說本世紀初期的歐洲劇場是易卜生的時代，那麼本世紀的五、六十年代無疑則是希萊希特的「史詩劇場」時代，那麼，什麼是「史詩劇場」呢？

西方的傳統劇場一向遵循亞里斯多德的理論，十七世紀法國的新古典主義時代更取其嚴格三一律規則來束縛劇場的表演，到了近代雖然產生較多變化，有自然主義、寫實主義及表現主義等等不同流派的表現方法，但萬變不離其宗，沒有人真正脫離亞里斯多德所樹立的那一套方針，即戲劇乃在反映真實的現實人生（藝術模仿人生的理論），戲劇的目的在於讓觀眾投入劇中事件或人物，藉以得到情感的洗滌，從劇場上對人生的模擬表演，進而真正感受到：這就是人生。一九二〇年代之際，希萊希特認為這種傳統的戲劇表現模式跟時代精神已經脫節了，他反而比較欣賞不隸屬於亞里斯多德系統的較為古老的東方劇場，特別是中國的史詩式及象徵式的表演方式，他甚至為此覺得十分著迷。

首先，他認為現代劇場應該是疏離的，觀眾在看戲的時候不應該入戲，不要把自己的情感完全投入，要提醒自己：你是在看戲，而不是在經驗人生。因此觀眾在看戲的時候要保持疏離態度，唯一必須做的就是思考，去想戲劇所要傳達的訊息是什麼。假若觀眾看戲的時候投入情感，認同劇中角色，為劇情所吸引，他便不能思考了，不能思考便無從產生批判態度，而這正是傳統劇作者和劇場導演所期待的觀眾反應，他們期待觀眾片時的臨場刺激，事後有沒有留下什麼比較深刻的印象，那就不是很重要了。布萊希特認為這種劇場和煮一餐好吃的菜請客實在沒什麼兩樣，因此就不客氣的稱之為「烹飪劇場」(culinary theatre)。

「史詩劇場」為達到疏離效果，其表演方式即要不斷提醒觀眾們眼前所發生的一切是虛幻的，他們坐在戲院裡正在觀看或傾聽過去在某一段時間某一個地方發生的某一件事情，而這件事情必然帶有某種教誨的意義，古希臘史詩或中國古代劇場即帶有這方面的功能，都在敘述故事，進而宣示倫理道德方面的教誨意義，其展現方式講究象徵手法，戲劇動作或甚至布景道具都以象徵方式呈現，我們會看到演員對觀眾自我介紹或說明他目前的處境或甚至內心的想法（《四川好女人》劇中開場序曲賣水的老王即是如此出場）。此外，劇中穿插歌唱藉以襯托劇情也是「史詩劇場」用來達到疏離效果的手段之一，因為這個方式違背寫實的原則，但有時卻也可能帶來意想不到的戲劇結果（比如《勇氣媽媽》劇中勇氣媽媽和大兒子在軍中重逢一幕用歌唱方式呈現就相當扣人心弦）。

事實上，要了解什麼是「史詩劇場」，《四川好女人》

一劇可以說是最典型的一例，這齣戲劇幾乎包括了「史詩劇場」的各種要素，它甚至以一種寓言的方式來抒發劇作者的教誨企圖，而且還把背景拉到作者似乎仍一知半解的中國社會（布萊希特起初一直以為四川是一個城市，後來有人告訴他了才知道四川原來是個省，面積和德國不相上下）。我們知道布萊希特是個有名的馬克思主義者，但他絕不是盲目唱和那一型，他很清楚社會改革有可能產生的矛盾後果，而他提倡的「史詩劇場」明顯正有此一企圖，因為他確信劇場絕非只是單純為了娛樂，他希望藉此宣揚他的思想，並用以教誨人心，他知道人的問題在哪裡，呈現人性的真正本質正是他的用心所在，《四川好女人》正是他對人性本質抱持疑惑態度的最直接宣言，而就戲劇形式的表達方面而言，可以說完全契合了他的「史詩劇場」的理論。

《四川好女人》一劇的主要命題是──如何印證在人的世界中行善的理論與實際，理論是，不管這個世界如何腐敗惡劣，只要有人願意行善，這個世界就有希望，值得維持下去。但實際卻是，行善的人最後卻倒了下去，行善帶來痛苦和傷害，因為這個世界上有太多的惡人和愚蠢之人。結論是，要改變人性或改變這個世界嗎？沒有人能夠給予答案，結尾的收場白如是說：「人與人之間要如何和睦相處，好人──包括女人──要有好報，一定要，一定要找出適當的方針，各位先生女士，幫我們找吧！」我們看得出來，這是一個千古以來找不出答案的寓言命題，人類的世界永遠存在著各式各樣的矛盾，想改變世界的企圖永遠不會成功，烏托邦永遠只是個理想，因為人性的矛盾永遠擺在那裡，是無法改變的。布萊希特透過寓言的方式

更為有力的將此一問題突顯出來，但他很清楚他不會有答案的。其實，在布萊希特的寓言故事裡，《四川好女人》和《高加索灰闌記》都揭示了一個共同的主題，那就是善良的誘惑，前者的妓女沈蒂，後者的婢女格路莎，她們都是本性善良憨厚的女人，結果想做好事的誘惑不斷對她們頻頻招手，這種人經常吃虧上當，被佔盡便宜，沈蒂即為此吃盡苦頭。其實，布萊希特的處世哲學觀是根本反對這種行為的，正如同他在《勇氣媽媽》和《伽利略》裡反對英雄主義一樣，人活著並不是為了逞強，而只是為了生活得更好而已。《四川好女人》一劇的寓言教訓是，行善值得稱頌，但必須量力而為，如同劇中妓女沈蒂所說：「不要別人痛苦，也不要自己痛苦，要別人幸福，也要自己幸福，這就是行善了。」意思就是說，凡事先考慮自己，行有餘力再去考慮別人；而且，要改變這個世界是不可能的，但可以作適度嘗試，同時公平和正義一定要加以維護。

這個劇本在表達形式上可以說是布萊希特真正嘗試中國式象徵表演方式的「史詩劇場」典型，我們看劇中沈蒂懷孕之後，想像帶著兒子散步時的默劇表演方式，簡直是京劇中象徵動作的精彩再版，同時也是默劇的至高形式的表現。此外，序曲中人物的自我介紹，劇中人物對觀眾發表批評意見，甚至歌唱等等，這些我們所熟悉的京劇表現方式，布萊希特在《四川好女人》一劇中均樂於引用，以期達到他所想要的「史詩劇場」效果。一般而言，這種劇場的戲劇創作形式不講究圓滿的邏輯結構，整個戲劇結構由許多個別的片段組合而成，其總體效果乃是建立在這些獨立片段的「並置」或「蒙太奇」等方式架構而成，分開來看，這些個別片段自成一體，但組合起來又是一個大的總體，這等原理其實跟中國古典戲劇也是非常相像的，其目的無非在於脫離寫實的作用而已。

總括而言，「史詩劇場」的基本前提是疏離的，手法是象徵的，目的是教誨的，而劇中大量引用歌唱更是傳統寫實劇場所沒有的，布萊希特以這些手段新創了一種有別於傳統的嶄新劇場形式，這種形式不久之後影響了前衛電影的表達方式，六十年代之際發軔的前衛電影不管是思想或表現手法可以說正是由「史詩劇場」延續而來，從某個角度看，「史詩劇場」竟也是現代主義運動中一支強勁的生力軍。

四川好女人

人物表

老王▶賣水者

三位神明

紳士

沈蒂／蕭大

辛太太

八口之家

失業者

木匠

房東太太梅珠

警察

年輕妓女

老妓女

楊森▶失業飛行員

理髮匠師傅

地毯店老闆及其妻

楊太太▶楊森之母

牧師

服務生

序曲

〔街道上，傍晚時分，賣水的人老王向觀眾自我介紹。〕

老　王　我在四川這一帶賣水，缺水的時候，我得跑老遠去取水，不缺水的時候，我就沒錢賺。可是，在我們省裡貧窮早已司空見慣，大家都說只有老天才能幫忙我們，一個四處奔波的買牛的人，我很高興從他那兒聽說，幾位大仙正下凡來到人間，此刻恐怕已經來到了四川。聽說天帝早有聽聞這裡怨聲載道，早就不勝其煩了。我在城門這兒少說已經等了三天，天色也快暗了，我可能會是第一個迎接他們的人，再晚一點，我恐怕就要錯失良機了，因為許多達官顯要會圍著他們，不斷提出種種請願。我要是能認出他們就好了！也許他們出現時不會走在一起，以免引人注意。那邊的一群人一定不是，他們剛剛下工（他看著幾個工人經過），他們的肩膀因為扛粗重的東西早已經歪斜了。那邊的一個傢伙也絕對不是，他的手指上面沾有墨水，他有可能是水泥工廠的辦公室職員。甚至那邊的兩位紳士也不像是大仙（兩個紳士走過去），他們看來好像常常在打人，仙人不會幹這種事。現在看那三個人！他們看起來很不一樣，他們看來營養良好，不像有職業，鞋上沾有塵土，可見必定來自遠方，他們一定就是大仙了。可憐我，大爺們！

〔老王一頭撲跪在他們面前。〕

神明甲　（高興）有人來迎接我們嗎？

老　王　（遞水給他們）已經等很久了，只有我知道你們要來。

神明甲　好，我們今晚需要過夜的地方，你知道哪裡可以過夜嗎？

老　王　過夜的地方？多的是！我們全鎮悉聽尊便，你們愛睡哪裡就睡哪裡，大爺！敢問您想在什麼樣的地方過夜？

〔神明們胸有成竹般的互相對望一下。〕

神明甲　就住最近的一家，孩子，試試最近的這一家看。

老　王　我有點怕只偏愛某一家會得罪其他有力人士，您知道，我寧可別人負我，不要我負別人。

神明甲　那麼，我們命令你，就住最近這一家！

老　王　那是何先生的家！請稍候一會兒！

〔他走向一間屋子，敲門，門開了，我們可以看到他被拒絕了，他走回來，猶豫不決的樣子。〕

老　王　真不巧，何先生不在家，他的僕人不敢作主，因為何先生一向很嚴厲，如果他知道被他拒絕的人是誰一定會暈倒，您說是不是？

眾神明　（微笑）那當然。

老　王　好吧，再等一下！隔壁是蘇寡婦的家，她會樂瘋了。（他跑向另一間屋子，可是很顯然又被拒絕了。）

老　王　我問過，她說她只有一個小房間，而且沒有整理，我知道她的屋子有些角落不太乾淨，她覺得不好意思，女人總是這樣，愛面子，我現在馬上去問曾先生家看看。

神明乙　小房間無所謂，告訴她我們這就過來了。

老　王　可是很髒，沒關係嗎？可能有很多蜘蛛。

神明乙 那無妨，有蜘蛛的地方，蒼蠅一定不多。

神明丙 不足掛慮，（友善地對老王）這樣吧，孩子，去問曾先生那裡，或別的地方，隨便哪裡都好，蜘蛛一向怕我。

〔老王敲另一家的門，屋裡的人讓他進去。〕

屋裡的聲音 求你的大仙們饒了我們吧！我們麻煩已經夠多了！

老　王 （回到眾神明那裡）曾先生很懊惱，他的屋子住滿了親戚，不敢出來見人，大爺！我猜想裡頭有些壞人，他不希望您老看到他們，他怕您責罰，事情就是這個樣子。

神明丙 我們那麼嚇人嗎？

老　王 只有壞人才怕，不是嗎？大家都知道，廣東省受水患之苦已經幾十年了，不是嗎？

神明乙 真的？為什麼？

老　王 嗯，因為他們不信宗教。

神明乙 胡說，那是因為他們沒建水壩。

神明甲 噓！（對老王）你還想再去問嗎？孩子？

老　王 您怎能這麼說呢？我只要再往前問另一間屋子就可以了，從那裡下去，你愛住哪裡就住哪裡，每個人都恨不得想巴結你們呢！剛才都是偶發狀況，您應該知道，我去！

〔他離開眾神明，然後站在街上，不知如何是好。〕

神明乙 我剛才說什麼？

神明丙 當然可能真的是「偶發狀況」。

神明乙 以前到貴州和廣東時，這次在四川，每次都是「偶發狀況」？現在已經沒有人信教了，這是赤裸裸的事實，你還是不願意面對，我們的任務已經失敗了，為什麼還不肯承認呢？

神明甲 我們可能隨時都會碰到一些好人，我們總不能期待事事如意吧。

神明丙 我們的決議是這樣：「只要有足夠的人活得像樣，這個世界就不需要改變。」換句話說，要有好人。如果我沒看錯，那個賣水的就是個好人。（他走向老王那裡，老王仍站著猶疑不決。）

神明乙 他看錯了，那個賣水的用度量杯取水給我們喝的時候，我注意到了不尋常的地方，杯子在這裡。（他拿杯子給神明甲看。）

神明甲 杯子有兩層底。

神明乙 騙子！

神明甲 好了，將他除名，一個人腐化，那有什麼關係？我們可以再找符合我們要求條件的人，我們勢必要找出一個！兩千年來，他們老是在叫：「這個世界非改變不可了，我們看不到永遠的好人。」現在機會來了，我們一定可以找到遵守我們的戒律的人。

神明丙 （對老王）要找個過夜的地方真的那麼困難嗎？

老　王 對你們而言不難！你們怎麼想的呢？你們無法立刻找到地方，這全是我的過錯，我沒有真正盡力。

神明丙 當然不是這樣。

〔說著走回去神明甲和神明乙那裡。〕

老　王 他們已經起疑心了，（他向一位紳士搭訕）對不起，這位仁兄，打擾您了，多年來整個四川都在談論三位大仙降臨的事情，現在他們真的來了，他們需要一個過夜的地方，不要走，看一下嘛，看在老天份上，就這一次，千載難逢的機會，趕快去要求他們去住你家，免得被別人捷足先登了，他們會接受的。

〔這位紳士不理會，走開離去。〕

老　王　（轉向另一個）親愛的先生，您已經聽到怎麼回事了吧？您府上大概有空房間吧？房間不必豪華，有誠意就夠了。

紳　士　我怎麼知道和你一道的是什麼樣的神？房子要給人住總得知道對方的來路吧。

〔他走進一家雜貨店，老王跑回眾神明那裡。〕

老　王　我已經找到一任紳士，他願意收留你們。

〔他看到他的杯子丟在地上，疑惑地看著眾神明，撿起杯子，然後又離開。〕

神明甲　這聽起來不像那麼回事。

老　王　（對著剛從雜貨店出來的紳士）房間沒問題吧？

紳　士　你怎麼不想我可能是住在客棧的？

神明甲　他吃憋了，我看我們把四川從名單上刪除吧。

老　王　他們是三位大仙哩！你不信教嗎？那麼漫不經心，會下油鍋的！神明會唾棄你！你會後悔！你要付出代價，你們這些人，沒有人能倖免，你們會給整個四川帶來不幸。（停頓），現在只剩妓女沈蒂了，她不會拒絕的。

〔他往上大叫「沈蒂」，沈蒂從窗口探頭出來。〕

老　王　他們來了，我找不到地方安頓他們，你今晚能不能收留他們？

沈　蒂　恐怕不行，老王，我在等一位客戶，你找不到別的地方了嗎？

老　王　現在說不清楚，四川真活像個大糞堆。

沈　蒂　我的客戶來時，我會躲起來，他看我不在大概會走開，他想帶我出場。

老　王　我們可以現在上來嗎？

沈　蒂　不要叫那麼大聲，要不要讓他們知道我是幹什麼的？

老　王　不！不能讓他們知道你的職業，我們還是在樓下等的好，你不會和你的客戶出去吧？

沈　蒂　我現在很拮据，如果明天付不出房租，會被趕走的。

老　王　我們現在沒有時間理會這些了。

沈　蒂　真是叫人為難，皇帝過生日，老百姓只好勒緊肚皮，好吧，我就收留他們。（我們可以看到她把燈火熄了。）

神明甲　我看像是沒搞頭。

〔他們走向老王。〕

老　王　（看到眾神明站在他背後，嚇了一跳）已經找到地方了。（說著用手拭汗。）

神　明　真的？可不可以先看看地方？

老　王　不急，慢慢來，房間還在整理。

神明丙　好吧，我們就坐在這兒等。

老　王　這裡的交通有點亂，要不要過去那邊？

神明乙　我們喜歡看人，這也正是我們來這裡的目的。

老　王　可是……那兒有輛拖車。

神明乙　喔，我們的身體很硬朗，用不著。

老　王　也許你們希望我帶你們看看四川的夜景？我們也可以四下走走。

神明丙　我們今天已經走夠多了，（微笑著）要是你不想我們待在這兒，請直說無妨。

〔他們走開。〕

神明丙　這樣可以了吧？

〔他們坐在一處門口台階上，老王隔著不遠處坐在地上。〕

老　王　（深深吸一口氣）你們今晚要和一位單身女子住在一塊，她是四川最好的女人，也是最好的人。

神明丙　這很好。

老　王　（對著觀眾）我剛才從地上拾起杯子的時候，他們看我的樣子可真怪，他們是不是已經注意到什麼了？我再也不敢正眼看他們了。

神明丙　你看起來疲憊不堪。

老　王　是有一點，跑路的關係。

神明甲　這裡的老百姓日子不好過嗎？

老　王　好人的日子不好過。

神明甲　（嚴肅地）你自己呢？

老　王　我知道你的意思，我不是好人，可是我的日子也並不好過。

〔這時一位紳士出現在沈蒂住屋的門口，他吹了幾聲口哨，每吹一聲口哨，老王就嚇一跳。〕

神明丙　（輕聲對老王）我猜那個人走了吧？

老　王　（迷惑）走了。

〔他起身跑向廣場，留下他的拐杖，這時紳士適巧離去，沈蒂走出門外，輕聲叫著「老王！」，然後走到街上。老王這時也叫著「沈蒂！」，但是沒有應聲。〕

老　王　她擺了我一道，大概去賺她的房租去了，我現在沒地方給那幾位大爺住了，他們看來已經很累了，還在那兒等著，我不能回去又告訴他們事情吹了。我自己那小地方，排水管，也不可能給他們住，何況他們也不會願意和一個已經被他們看穿了有不誠實行為的人住一起，我沒有臉再去見他們，可是拐杖還丟在那兒，我該怎麼辦呢？我不敢回去拿，既然不能為我所尊敬的神明們做任何事情，看來只有離開四川一途，不要讓他們再見到我。

〔他匆忙離去，沈蒂回來，她走向一旁尋找老王，卻見到了眾神明。〕

沈　蒂　敢問你們就是神明大爺們？我叫做沈蒂，要是您不嫌棄我的小房間，那我真是不勝榮幸之至。

神明丙　賣水的人怎麼不見了？

沈　蒂　我可能和他互相錯過了。

神明甲　他大概以為你不來了，不敢回來稟報，溜掉了。

神明丙　（撿起地上的拐杖）我們把這個放在你這裡，他會回來拿的。

〔沈蒂引領眾神明進入她的屋子，天色已暗，燈又亮了起來。黎明來臨，沈蒂點著燈籠，引領眾神明走出門外，他們準備離去。〕

神明甲 親愛的沈蒂，你的熱誠招待，我們真是感激不盡，我們不會忘記你曾經收留我們，把這支拐杖還給那位賣水的人，代我們謝謝他讓我們知道這個世界上有你這樣一個好人。

沈　蒂 我不是好人，我必須承認，當老王要求我收留你們時，我猶豫不決。

神明甲 猶豫不決沒什麼關係，你最後畢竟還是做了，你要知道，你所做的不只是提供給我們睡著的地方而已，許多人——包括我們神明在內——始終在懷疑這世界上是否還有好人存在，我們這趟旅行的目的就是在尋找這個答案，現在我們找到了，我們可以很高興繼續上路，再見！

沈　蒂 慢著，大爺們！我不敢確定我是不是好人，當然我希望做好人，可是我怎麼付我的房租呢？好吧，我只好向你們坦白，我為了求生存而出賣自己，但即使如此，也還是過不下去，我知道很多人跟我一樣，我為了活下去什麼事都願意做，誰不是呢？我以我父母的榮譽說實話，我不會去羨慕鄰居有好房子住，要是我能嫁個男人並從一而終，我會很高興，我不希望剝削別人，也不會去欺負弱者，可是，我該如何做？怎麼做呢？我只不過打破幾個戒律而已，卻幾乎已經活不下去了。

神明甲 沈蒂，你講的這些，都是一個好女人必然會有的疑慮。

神明丙 再會，沈蒂，代我們問候賣水的人，他是我們的好朋友。

神明乙 我看他的情況也好不到哪裡。

神明丙 祝你好運！

神明甲 最重要的，做好人，沈蒂，再會！

〔他仍轉身準備要走，已經開始揮手。〕

沈　蒂　（憂慮的樣子）可是我不知道該怎麼辦，大爺們！物價這麼昂貴，我怎麼做好人呢？

神明乙　我們也是無能為力，我們無法干涉經濟事務。

神明丙　慢著！等一下！如果讓她稍微有錢一點，日子會不會好過些？

神明乙　我們不能給她什麼，我們無法跟上面報帳。

神明甲　為什麼不行？

〔三個人交頭接耳，興奮地談著。〕

神明甲　（難為情地，對沈蒂）你說你付不出房租，我們不是乞丐，住了你的房子，我們該付房租才對，這個拿去！（他給她錢）不要跟任何人說我們付給你錢，免得引起誤會。

神明乙　這極可能引起誤會。

神明甲　但合法，我們住房子付租金，沒什麼好誤會的，何況也沒有抵觸我們的決議。好吧，再見！

〔眾神明迅速離去。〕

第一場

〔一間小煙草店，店裡尚未完全裝潢好，店門還關著。〕

沈　蒂　（對著觀眾）神明大爺們離開這裡已經三天了，臨走時他們說要付給我過夜的租金，我仔細一看，居然是一千多塊錢大洋，有了這筆錢，我就買下了這煙草店，昨天才剛搬進來，我希望現在能夠好好做些善事。說著這家店的舊主人辛太太來了，她昨天來跟我要一些米，說是要煮給小孩吃的。現在我看見她捧著缽經過廣場往這兒來了。

〔辛太太走進來，兩個女人互相鞠躬。〕

沈　蒂　早，辛太太。

辛太太　早，沈蒂小姐，搬進這個新家還喜歡吧？

沈　蒂　非常喜歡，夜裡孩子們還好吧？

辛太太　喔，親愛的，住進新房子，如果木板屋也可以叫做房子的話！小的夜裡一直咳個不停。

沈　蒂　那可真糟。

辛太太　你不知道什麼叫做糟，你現在可闊了，不過，在這鬼地方你慢慢會學些東西的，這一帶可稱得上是個貧民窟呢！

沈　蒂　你沒告訴我水泥工廠的工人中午都會來這兒？

辛太太　是啊，要不然誰會來這兒買東西？附近的人才不會呢！

沈　蒂　你賣店給我時沒告訴我這些。

辛太太　別開始怪我了，首先，你從我和我的小孩手中弄走這家站舖，然後說這是個鬼地方，是個貧民窟，真沒天良！（她開始哭。）

沈　蒂　（很快的）你要的米我趕快弄給你。

辛太太　我還想跟你借點錢。

沈　蒂　（把米倒進缽裡）我沒錢借，你知道我還沒開始做生意哩！

辛太太　可是我需要錢用，我要靠什麼過活？我什麼東西都給你拿走了，你現在還要趕盡殺絕！我要把小孩丟在你家門口，你這殺千刀的！（她從沈蒂手裡把缽搶過來。）

沈　蒂　別生氣！你會把米灑掉！

〔一對老夫妻和一個衣著襤褸的年輕人走進來。〕

妻　子　喔，我親愛的沈蒂，我們聽說你現在發了，你已經成為女生意人啦！你一定想不到，我們的雜貨店已經倒閉了，我們現在無家可歸，不知可不可以在你這兒暫借住一個晚上。認識我外甥吧？他也來了，他一向都是和我們一道的。

外　甥　（四周張望）好漂亮的店！

辛太太　這些人是誰啊？

沈　蒂　我當初從鄉下來的時候，他們收留過我。（對觀眾）可是當我僅有的一點錢用完之後，就把我掃地出門，也許他們現在正擔心我會拒絕他們。

他們窮，
他們沒地方住，
他們沒有朋友，
他們要人幫忙，
你怎能說不？

（對著這三個剛進來的人，很友善地）歡迎！我很高興給你們住的地方，可是我只有一個很小的房間，就在店的後面。

丈　夫　那夠了，不用操心。

妻　子　（給沈蒂一杯茶）我們最好住後面，免得礙手礙腳的。我猜你選擇開煙草店是為了紀念你的第一個家，我們可以給你一些建議，這是我們來這裡的另一個理由。

辛太太　（冷笑）我希望顧客也會跟著上門。

妻　子　我們就是顧客。

丈　夫　噓，有一個顧客上門來了。

〔進來一個衣衫襤褸的人。〕

衣衫襤褸者　對不起，我失業了。

〔辛太太笑。〕

沈　蒂　我能為你效勞嗎？

衣衫襤褸者　我聽說你明天開張，有些東西不趕緊開包會很容易壞掉的，可不可以給我一根香煙？

妻　子　神經，跟人要香煙！他至少應該要麵包吧！

衣衫襤褸者　麵包很貴，我只要吐幾口煙，精神就來了，變成另一個人。

沈　蒂　（給他一些香煙）有精神很重要，你將是我的店開張的第一個顧客，你會給我帶來好運。

〔衣衫襤褸者很快點燃一根香煙，猛吸一口，咳著走出去。〕

妻　子　我親愛的沈蒂，你這樣做對嗎？

辛太太　照你這個方式開店，三天之內一定關門大吉。

丈　夫　我敢打賭剛才那傢伙口袋裡一定還有錢。

沈　蒂　但他說他沒錢。

外　甥　你怎麼知道他不是在說謊？

沈　蒂　（生氣）我怎麼知道他是在說謊？

妻　子　（搖頭）她不懂得拒絕別人！你太善良了，沈蒂，你如果要保有這家店，你就要時時學習怎麼拒絕別人。

丈　夫　你為什麼不說店不是你的，是一位親戚的，老闆要求帳目清楚，你做不到這個嗎？

辛太太　只要不老是想當好人就可以做得到。

沈　蒂　（笑）嘮叨，嘮叨，嘮叨！如果你不收斂著點，告訴你，我要把給你的米收回。

妻　子　（嚇一跳）米也是你的嗎？

沈　蒂　（對著觀眾）

他們壞，
他們沒有朋友，
他們捨不得給人米，
他們什麼都要，
誰能說他們不是？

〔進來一個小個子的人。〕

辛太太　（看到小個子進來，急著要走）我明天再來看你。（退場。）

小個子　（在後面叫她）慢著，辛太太！我正在找你。

妻　子　她經常來嗎？她是不是對你有什麼索求？

沈　蒂　她沒什麼索求，她只是餓而已，這比索求什麼還糟。

小個子　她知道她為什麼要跑，你是新店主嗎？喔，架上又塞滿東西了，可惜這些都不屬於你，瞧！除非你先付錢，先前這裡的幾個王八蛋沒有人付過錢。（對著其他人）知道吧，我是木匠。

沈　蒂　我以為這些東西包括在裝潢裡面，我已經付過錢了。

木　匠　騙人！全是騙人！你和那位姓辛的女人是一夥的，我要求我的一百塊大洋，我叫林吐。

沈　蒂　我怎麼給你錢？我已經沒有多餘的錢了！

木　匠　那麼，我要逮捕你，馬上給錢，要不然就逮捕你。

丈　夫　（推沈蒂一下）表哥！

沈　蒂　能不能下個月再給你錢？

木　匠　（吼叫）不行！

沈　蒂　不要那麼強硬，林吐先生，我無法一口氣處理那麼多事情。

（對著觀眾）

小小的放縱，力量可以加倍，

瞧，讓拉車的馬停下來嗅嗅草，

縱容一下，馬可以拉車拉得更好。

六月裡的一點耐心，到了八月樹上

就會結滿桃子。

沒有耐心我們怎麼住在一起？

短暫的拖延，才能達到更遠的目標。

（對著木匠）再忍耐一陣子吧，林吐先生！

木　匠　可是誰要對我和我的家人有耐心呢？（他從牆上移下一個架子，好像準備要帶走），給錢，要不然我要把這些架子統統帶走！

妻　子　我親愛的沈蒂，何不讓你表哥來處理這件事情？（對著木匠）寫下你的聲明吧，沈蒂小姐的表哥會付你錢。

木　匠　表哥！這些表哥們！

外　甥　不要笑成那個樣子，我私下認識他。

丈　夫　他是條漢子！精明得像把刀！

木　匠　好吧，他會收到我的帳單！（他放下一個架子，坐在架子上面，寫下他的帳單。）

妻　子　（對沈蒂）如果你不阻止他，他會連你身上的衣服都剝光。不要承認任何聲明，否則你會吃不完兜著走，好比你丟一塊肉到垃圾筒，這附近所有的髒狗就會統統湧來你家的後院，我們的法院不知道是幹什麼用的？

沈　蒂　如果他的工作沒辦法供養他，法院也無能為力，他在這裡幹了些活兒，自然不肯空著手回去，他有家庭要養，可惜我無法付他錢，真不知道那些神明大爺們要怎麼說？

丈　夫　你收留我們，已經算是仁至義盡，很夠意思了。（進來一個跛腳的男人和一個懷孕的女人。）

跛腳者　（對著那對老夫妻）喔，你們在這兒！你們真是好親戚呀！把我們丟在街角。

妻　子　（尷尬樣子，對沈蒂）這是我的弟弟，姓翁，另外這位是弟媳。（對他們兩人）不要抱怨吧，到一旁靜靜坐著，不要打擾我們的老朋友沈蒂小姐。你們可以待在這兒，她不會反對的。（對沈蒂）我看我們得收留他們兩人，我的弟媳有五個月身孕了，你不反對吧？

沈　蒂　喔，不會，歡迎！

妻　子　（對著兩人）說聲謝謝，杯子在後面。（對沈蒂）他們就是沒地方去，還好你開了一家店！

沈　蒂　（笑著，手上拿著茶，對著觀眾）是啊，我幹了好一樁善事！

〔進來房東太太梅珠，手上拿著一張空白表格。〕

房東太太　沈蒂小姐，我是你的房東梅珠太太，我希望我們可以處得來，這個是租約。（沈蒂拿過租約讀）開家小店真不錯，可不是嗎？諸位先生女士們，（他環顧四周）我看架上的東西好像還沒裝滿，不過那倒沒什麼關係，你可不可以給我幾個擔保人？

沈　蒂　有必要嗎？

房東太太　我對你的底細不清楚。

丈　夫　也許我們可以給沈蒂小姐擔保吧？她初來鎮上時我們就認識了，我們可以隨時為她赴湯蹈火。

房東太太　你是誰啊？

丈　夫　我是煙草商，叫馬虎。

房東太太　你的店在哪裡？

丈　夫　我現在沒開店，賣了。

房東太太　原來如此，（對沈蒂）你還認識其他可以告訴我有關你背景的人嗎？

妻　子　（提醒沈蒂）表哥！表哥！

房東太太　你要租我的房子，非得有人為你擔保不可，我這房子可是很體面的，沒有擔保，我無法跟你簽租約。

沈　蒂　（慢慢地，眼睛往下望）我有一位表哥。

房東太太　喔，你有一位表哥，就住廣場這一帶？我們可以馬上過去，他是做什麼的？

沈　蒂　他不住在這裡，他住別的城鎮。

妻　子　你可不是說他是住在松江吧？

沈　蒂　是住在松江，他……他叫蕭大先生。

丈　夫　我認識他！是不是高高瘦瘦的？

外　甥　（對著木匠）你也要和沈蒂的表哥接頭的！那些架子的事情！

木　匠　（語氣肯定）我正在寫要給他的帳單，寫好了！（把寫好的帳單遞出來）明天早上我會再回來。（退場）

外　甥　（在後面叫他，看了房東太太一眼）不用操心，表哥會付你

錢的！

房東太太　（仔細看著沈蒂）好吧！我會很高興和他見面，早安！（退場）

妻　子　（停頓一下）貓兒已經溜出布袋了，想必明早她就會知道你的底細了。

弟媳婦　（輕聲對外甥）紙是包不住火的！

〔進來一位男孩，牽著一位老人。〕

男　孩　（叫著）大家都來了。

妻　子　晚安，爺爺，（對沈蒂）好一位老者！他一定很擔心我們，還有這個男孩，已經長大啦？他很會吃，好了，老天，你還帶了誰來？

丈　夫　（往外看）只有我們的姪女。

弟媳婦　（輕聲對外甥，這時一位年輕女孩進來）所有的老鼠都爬進一條要沈的船了！

妻　子　（對沈蒂）這是鄉下來的一位年輕親戚，我希望我們的人數不會太多，你以前住我們那裡時，人沒這麼多吧？是啊，我們的人現在是多了些。現在可真的是粥少僧多了，再不把門鎖上，等一下就不得安寧（她鎖上門，大家都坐下來），最重要的是，我們絕不能干擾到你的生意，不做生意，我們要依靠什麼？我看我們來這樣安排事情，白天的時候年輕人都出去，家裡只留爺爺，弟媳婦，也許還有我自己，大家沒事就盡量回來關照一下，這樣可以吧？把那邊的燈點亮，大家自在些，不要拘束。

外　甥　（幽默）但願表哥今晚不要突然出現，我們嚴厲的蕭大先生！

〔弟媳婦笑。〕

弟　弟　（伸手拿香煙）拿支香煙應該沒多大關係。

丈　夫　我敢說絕對不會。

〔大家自己拿香煙，弟弟還伸手拿了一壺酒。〕

外　甥　表哥會付帳的。

爺　爺　（嚴肅地對著沈蒂）晚安！

〔沈蒂為這遲來的致意感到困惑，鞠躬，一手拿著木匠給她的帳單，另一手拿著租約。〕

妻　子　能不能唱支歌來娛樂一下我們的女主人？

外　甥　由爺爺開始！

〔大家唱歌〕

「煙之歌」

爺　爺　從前——我還沒老，頭髮還沒變白的時候——
我以為只要聰明就可以活得下去，
可是什麼時候聰明填飽過窮人的肚皮？沒有！沒有！
所以我才說：算了吧！
望著灰色的煙飄著，
飄向冷冷的寒氣，所以
啟航划行吧。

丈　夫　我看到誠實有良心的人被壓迫，

我只好走上彎曲的小路，
可是小路還是帶領我們走下坡，
要怎麼辦我實在不知道，
所以我只好說：算了吧！
望著灰白的煙飄著，
飄向冷冷的寒氣，所以
啟航划行吧。

姪　女　我聽說老一輩已經沒什麼好指望了，
既然時間可以治癒一切，治療他們吧，
可是我又聽說大門正為年輕人敞開著，
他們卻告訴我，門開了，什麼都沒有，
所以我只好說：算了吧！
望著灰白的煙飄著，
飄向冷冷的寒氣，所以
啟航划行吧。

外　甥　你從哪裡弄到這酒的？

弟媳婦　他把那袋煙草拿去當了。

丈　夫　什麼？那袋煙草是我們剩下的僅有的！我們不敢動它，那是要付房租的啊！你這豬！

弟　弟　你罵我豬，是因為我太太冷酷是嗎？你自己都在喝酒？把酒壺給我！

〔兩個人扭打，架子倒了下來。〕

沈　蒂　（哀求他們）喔，饒了我的店吧！不要糟蹋東西，這是神明給的禮物！要什麼儘管拿，就是不要糟蹋！

妻　子　（以懷疑口氣）這家店比我所想的還要小，我看最好不要讓阿姨和其他人也知道，免得他們也來了，擠不下。

弟媳婦　我們的女主人冷靜下來了。

〔外面傳來聲音，有人敲門。〕

外面聲音　開門！是我們！

妻　子　是阿姨嗎？我們怎麼辦？

沈　蒂　喔，希望！我漂亮的店！昨天才買下來的店，今天就這樣完了。

這個小救生艇
這麼快就下沈了
太多人貪婪地搶著上來
大家只好沈下去淹死算了。

外面聲音　開門！

第一場 A

〔橋下，賣水的人蹲在河旁。〕

老　王　（四周張望）好安靜，我已經躲了四天了，他們找不到我，因為我隨時提高警覺，我故意跟在他們後面走。第二天的時候，他們經過這座橋，我聽到了他們的腳步聲，現在他們大概已經走遠了，我這會兒應該是安全了。

〔他往後躺下，睡著了。音樂聲起，斜坡變成透明，眾神明出現。〕

老　王　（抬起一隻手臂擋臉，好像有人要打他）不要提了！我知道一切了！我找不到人願意收留你們，沒有一家願意！現在你們知道了！你們可以繼續上路了！

神明甲　可是你有找到一個願意收留我們的人，你走開的時候，她來了，她收留我們過夜，還為我們守夜，早晨我們離開的時候，她還點燈為我們照路，你說過她是個好女人，她是真的好。

老　王　這麼說來沈蒂真的收留你們了？

神明丙　當然。

老　王　我當時那麼沒信心，竟逃跑了！因為那時我這樣想:「她不會來的，因為她很拮据，她不會來的。」

眾神明

喔，軟弱的傢伙！
喔，好性情卻是個軟弱的人！
他想，有需要的時候，就沒有善良！
他想，有危險的時候，就沒有勇氣！

喔，軟弱總是相信最糟的事情！

喔，匆忙的判斷！草率的絕望！

老　王　我真丟臉，大爺們！

神明甲　現在，賣水的人，幫我們點忙，趕快回去四川，去找沈蒂，然後再跟我們報告她的情況。她現在闊了，她開了家小店，應該賺了些錢，可以了遂行善的心願。對她的善良表現一點興趣，沒有人是永遠善良的，特別是當善良不被需要的時候。我們要繼續旅行，我們要繼續尋找和四川好女人一樣的人們，我們老是在談論這世界上沒有好人，以後就不再談這些了。（他們消失）

第二場

〔煙草店內，大家四處睡著，燈還在燃燒，敲門聲。〕

妻　子　（爬起，睡眼惺忪）沈蒂！有人在敲門！咦，她哪裡去了？

外　甥　我猜她正在做早餐，表哥會付錢的！

〔妻子笑，拖著腳步去開門，一位年輕人進來，後面跟著木匠。〕

年輕人　我是表哥。

妻　子　（驚醒，不知所措）什麼？！

年輕人　我叫做蕭大。

眾　人　（互相搖醒）她的表哥！那是開玩笑，她哪有表哥！現在居然有人說是她的表哥！這麼大清早，沒有人相信！

外　甥　如果你真的是我們女主人的表哥，趕快去幫我們弄早餐來！

蕭　大　（把燈弄熄）第一批顧客就要上門來了，請趕快穿好衣服，這樣我的店才能開門。

丈　夫　你的店？我猜這店應該是我們的朋友沈蒂的。（蕭大搖搖頭）什麼？這根本不是她的店？

弟媳婦　這麼說來，她騙了我們！咦，她人哪兒去了？

蕭　大　她被耽擱著，現在我來了，她要我告訴你們，從現在起她再也不能為你們做任何事情了。

妻　子　（深受震撼）我們都以為她是好人呢！

外　甥　不要相信他的話，我們找她！

丈　夫　我們這就去找，（他開始指揮）你和你，還有你以及你，你們分頭四處去找，爺爺和我們留守總部，同時男孩趁這機會給大家弄吃的，（對男孩）你看到街角的那家麵包店沒有？偷偷過去，把襯衫塞滿。

弟媳婦 順便也拿些小蛋糕！

丈　夫 可是要小心，別讓麵包師逮著你了！還有，也別撞上了警察！

〔男孩點頭，然後離去，其他人也都穿好了衣服。〕

蕭　大 這家店是你們的避難所，你們去偷麵包店，不怕給這裡帶來惡名嗎？

外　甥 別理他，我們很快就會找到沈蒂，她會把事情跟他說清楚。

〔外甥、弟弟、弟媳婦以及姪女等人出去。〕

弟媳婦 （離去時）別忘了留點早餐給我們！

蕭　大 （冷靜）你們找不到她的，我的表妹不能漫無節制款待你們，她覺得很遺憾，不幸的是你們人實在太多了，這只是一家小煙草店，沈蒂小姐要依賴這個過生活。

丈　夫 我們的沈蒂絕不會講這種話。

蕭　大 也許你是對的，（對木匠）在這個城市裡，一個人無法應付那麼多的要求，這真是不幸，看來一千一百年前有人說過的這個故事，至今仍然是真的，他的故事是這樣的：
有人問縣長要怎樣幫助鎮上受凍的人們，
他回答說：
「一條一萬呎長的棉被
就可以連郊區都蓋到了。

〔他開始清理店內。〕

木　匠　我看你正在幫你表妹整理事務，這裡有筆小債務，有旁人為證，我們必須處理一下，這些架子，一百塊大洋。

蕭　大　（從口袋拿出帳單，友善地）一百塊大洋不會太貴了一些嗎？

木　匠　不，我無法減價，我有老婆和小孩要養。

蕭　大　（嚴肅地）你有幾個小孩？

木　匠　四個。

蕭　大　那麼我給你二十塊大洋。

〔丈夫笑。〕

木　匠　你瘋了嗎？這些架子可是胡桃木做的！

蕭　大　那你帶走吧。

木　匠　你什麼意思？

蕭　大　太貴了，請你把你的胡桃木架子帶走吧。

妻　子　說得好！（她也笑了。）

木　匠　（不確定地）趕快把沈蒂找來，她似乎比你好些。

蕭　大　當然，她因此被糟蹋了。

木　匠　（堅定地拿著幾個架子走向門口）你就把你的貨物都堆在地上吧！算我倒霉！

蕭　大　（對著丈夫）幫他忙！

丈　夫　（抓了一個架子走向門口，露齒笑著）帶著這些架子滾吧！

木　匠　你們這些狗，你們要我老婆小孩餓死是嗎？

蕭　大　再一次，我出價二十塊大洋，我也不想把我的貨物堆在地上。

木　匠　一百！

〔蕭大冷漠地望著窗外，丈夫正準備把更多的架子拿出去。〕

木　匠　拜託不要把架子扔向門柱吧，白痴！（絕望的）這些架子都是按尺寸大小做的，只適合這個鬼地方而已！木板弄壞了，先生！

蕭　大　正是，出價二十塊大洋，就是因為木板壞了。

〔妻子快樂地哀叫著。〕

木　匠　（突然露出倦怠）留著這些架子也沒用，就照你出的價錢吧！

蕭　大　二十塊大洋。

〔他把兩個大銅板放到桌上，木匠收下。〕

丈　夫　（把架子拿回來）一堆破木板，那是夠了。木匠去好好喝醉一番，也許是真的夠了！（退場）

丈　夫　終於把他擺脫掉了！

妻　子　（哭得很高興，還一邊擦眼淚）「這是胡桃木做的！」「那你帶走吧！」「一百塊大洋！我有四個小孩！」「我只能出價二十！」「這些木板都壞了！」「正是！二十塊大洋！」——這就是我們對付無賴的方式。

蕭　大　是的。（熱切地）趕快滾蛋！

丈　夫　我們？

蕭　大　是的，你們，你們這些賊和寄生蟲，如果你們趕快滾，不要再饒舌，你們還可能有救。

丈　夫　最好別理會他，不要和餓肚子的人吵嘴，我只是想知道，男孩到底去了哪裡。

蕭　大　是啊，男孩呢？我說過了，他偷了蛋糕，我就不讓他進這店。（突然大喊）再一次，滾！

〔大家仍坐著不動〕

蕭　大　（冷靜地）隨便你們。

〔他走向門口，彎腰鞠躬，一個警察出現在門口。〕

蕭　大　想必您是這附近管區的大爺？

警　察　正是，先生您是……

蕭　大　蕭大（大家笑），今天天氣真好！

警　察　熱了些，可不是？

蕭　大　是熱了些，是的。

丈　夫　（輕輕地對妻子）如果他再這樣囉嗦下去，等男孩回來時，我們就完蛋了！

〔他想和蕭大打暗號。〕

蕭　大　（不理會他）店裡比較涼爽，街上有灰塵，不同的場所，對天氣的感覺就會不一樣。

警　察　非常的不一樣。

妻　子　（對著丈夫）不要擔心，男孩看到警察站在門口，不會進來的。

蕭　大　要不要進來？裡頭倒是真的涼爽些，我和我表妹剛開了這家店，坦白說，我們倒很想和官廳打些交道哩。

警　察　（走進來）您真客氣，蕭大先生，是啊，裡頭是真的比較涼爽。

丈　夫　（輕聲地）他讓他進來，這下子好了，等一下男孩回來時就注意不到他了。

蕭　大　這些人是我們的訪客，聽我表妹說，是她遠方的熟朋友，他們在旅行，（大家鞠躬）就要走了。

丈　夫　（粗聲地）是的，我們現在正準備要走。

蕭　大　我會告訴我表妹，說你們等不及她回來，不能當面跟她道謝。

〔街上傳來「抓賊」喊叫聲。〕

警　察　怎麼回事？

〔男孩出現在門口，各式各樣的蛋糕從他的襯衫裡掉出來，妻子氣急敗壞地跟他揮手不要他進來，他轉身正要走。〕

警　察　你給我站住！（他抓住男孩）這些蛋糕哪裡弄來的？

男　孩　那邊。

警　察　喔，偷的，對不對？

妻　子　這不關我們的事，這男孩他自己幹的。（對男孩）你這沒用的東西！

警　察　蕭大先生，您能不能解釋一下這到底是怎麼回事？

〔蕭大不吭聲。〕

警　察　啊，哈，你們統統跟我到局裡去。

蕭　大　我店裡會發生這種事，真是叫人難堪。

妻　子　剛才男孩要跑掉時，他坐視不管。

蕭　大　我要聲明的是，大人，如果我要藏匿小偷，剛才就沒有必要請您進來了。

警　察　沒錯，不過，蕭大先生，你必須諒解一點，職責所在，我還是

必須把這些人帶走，（蕭大鞠躬）走！（他把眾人帶走。）

爺　爺　（在門口嚴肅地）日安！

〔除了蕭大，所有人均退場，他繼續清理，房東太太進來。〕

房東太太　你就是她的表哥！警察從我的房子裡帶走一堆人，這是怎麼回事？你的沈蒂小姐有什麼權利把這個店變成收容所？昨天住廉價旅館，今天去街角麵包店跟人家乞討麵包，你看，收容這樣的人會有什麼樣的下場？我早就知道！

蕭　大　是的，我了解，有人跟你講許多她的壞話，有人說她曾經餓肚子，說她生活窘困實在很離譜，她最壞的名聲就是：窮。

房東太太　她是個普通……

蕭　大　乞丐，不要把話扭曲了。

房東太太　喔，不要那麼濫情無聊，我在談她的行為，而不是她的收入，當然她一定有相當收入，要不然怎麼會有這家店。我知這有幾個老紳士給她錢，要不然要弄一間這樣的店談何容易？先生，這是一棟很像樣的房子，有許多人同時在這裡租住，他們可不會喜歡和這樣的人住在同一個屋簷下，先生，（停頓）我不是故意刁難，我只是必須謹滇。

蕭　大　（冷淡地）梅珠太太，我很忙，請你直接告訴我，住在這麼像樣的房子裡，我們要給多少錢才行。

房東太太　我不得不說，你是個冷酷的房客。

蕭　大　（從櫃台拿出租約）房租很高，合約上說，我們是按月付房租。

房東太太　（很快地）像你表妹這樣的人可不行！

蕭　大　什麼意思？

房東太太　我的意思是說，像你表妹這樣的人必須半年一付，兩百塊大洋，事先一次付清。

蕭　大　兩百塊大洋！這簡直是敲詐！我那來那麼多錢？我又不能期待這個店馬上大發利市，我唯一的希望是寄望在水泥廠裡製造袋子的工人，聽說他們的工作很累人，所以都抽很多煙，但是他們賺的錢卻又不多。

房東太太　你應該早就想到這個。

蕭　大　梅珠太太，有點良心吧！沒錯，我表妹不該讓那些不幸的傢伙進來住，這很不應該，但她會改進的，我保證她一定會改進，而且，她出身寒微，她了解什麼是貧窮，有比這更好的房客嗎？她會賣力工作，準時付房租，她會做任何事情，犧牲一切，賣任何東西，不規避責任，她會像小老鼠一般溫馴，像蒼蠅一樣安靜，她租你房子的一天，就會完全配合你的要求，這樣的房客真的是沒處找了。

房東太太　預付兩百塊大洋，否則就請她回去街上幹老勾當！

〔警察進來。〕

警　察　希望沒打擾到你們，蕭大先生！

房東太太　想必警方對這家店一定很感興趣。

警　察　梅珠太太，你這樣說就不對了，蕭大先生幫了我們一點小忙，我只是代表警方來跟他道聲謝。

房東太太　好吧，這不關我的事。蕭大先生，我希望我的提議你表妹不會有意見，我喜歡和房客們好來好往，日安，兩位先生。（退場）

蕭　大　日安，梅珠太太。

警　察　你是不是和梅珠太太有點麻煩？

蕭　大　她要求我們預付房租，因為她覺得我的表妹跟她這棟像樣的房子不太配。

警　察　你沒錢付對不對？（蕭大沈默不語）可是像你這樣的人，蕭大先生，應該不難借到錢吧？

蕭　大　也許，可是像沈蒂那樣的女人要去哪裡借錢？

警　察　你會留下來吧？

蕭　大　不，而且走了之後也不會再回來，我剛好路過這裡，只能幫她一下子而已，頂多處理最棘手的部份，以後就要靠她自己了，不知道未來會變成怎樣，我很擔心。

警　察　蕭大先生，很遺憾你有付房租的困難，我不得不承認起初我們都以很複雜的眼光來看這家店，但是剛才你那英勇的行為，令我非常佩服，當局不久就會發現你是個值得信賴的人。

蕭　大　（痛苦地）大人，我表妹把這間小店看成是神明送給她的禮物，我不能讓它斷送掉，我預備盡我所能不顧一切去維護這些，可是老天總是和弱者作對，命運也喜歡捉弄人，我覺得自己像是在照應一群老鼠，老是在帶領牠們渡河，（停頓一會兒）你抽煙吧？

警　察　（拿了兩根香煙進口袋裡）我們局裡的同事都希望你不要走，蕭大先生，可是你應該了解梅珠太太這個人，沈蒂——我們不用拐彎抹角——以出賣皮肉維生，你可能會說：她能做什麼呢？她不做這個她用什麼去付房租呢？可是問題是：幹這種勾當並不光彩。為什麼呢？第一，人不能出賣愛——能賣的愛就得特別提防了！第二，如果你愛某人，你和他在一起，這是光彩的事情，可是如果付你錢你才跟他在一起，這就不一樣了。第三，俗話說：只要愛情，不要麵包。好，你會說，當牛奶潑掉的時候，這句話有什麼意義呢？她該怎麼辦呢？她必須想辦法弄到半年的房租，要不然就回到街上去幹老勾當，她怎樣才能弄到房租呢？蕭大先生，坦白說，我不知道，（他不斷想著）蕭大先生，我想到了！給她找位丈夫！

〔一個矮小的老婦人進來。〕

老婦人 我要給我丈夫買支便宜的好雪茄，到明天我們就結婚四十年了，瞧，我們要小小慶祝一番。

蕭　大 （禮貌地）四十年了，還想慶祝！

老婦人 我們能力所及，為什麼不？我們在對面開了一家地毯店，希望我們做好鄰居，應該不成問題，時機真壞。

蕭　大 （拿幾個盒子給她看）那恐怕已經是老生常談了。

警　察 蕭大先生，我們需要一筆錢，好，我來湊合一樁婚姻。

蕭　大 （對著老婦人，露出歉意）很不好意思，我正拿我自己的問題在麻煩這位先生。

警　察 我們付不出半年的房租，很好，我們想靠結婚來弄一小筆錢。

蕭　大 這恐怕不容易。

警　察 怎麼會？她是個好對象，她有一間前途看好的小店，（對老婦人）你認為怎麼樣？

老婦人 （決定不下）是……。

警　察 在報紙上刊登徵婚啟事！

老婦人 （沈靜地）如果那位年輕小姐同意的話……。

警　察 她有什麼好不同意的？我來處理啟事的事情，好心會有好報，不要以為當局從不關心小生意人的死活，你幫了我們一次小忙，我就為你擬一則徵婚啟事，哈！哈！哈！

〔他很熱心地拿出一本筆記簿，沾濕鉛筆的筆心，開始寫。〕

蕭　大　（慢慢地）這主意倒不錯。

警　察　「有否任何……小有資產的……品行端正人士……包括鰥夫……願意入贅於一……生意興隆之煙草店？」然後再補上：「敝人容貌美麗……個性宜人。」怎麼樣？

蕭　大　好像是太誇張了一點……。

老婦人　（和善地）一點也不，我看過她的人。

〔警察從筆記簿上撕下這張紙，交給蕭大。〕

蕭　大　一想到要讓事情行得通，要那麼依賴運氣，我就覺得惶恐。那麼多的主意！那麼多的朋友！（對警察）關於店裡房租的事情，我已經使盡全力，還是無能為力，然後你來了，給我出這麼好的主意，坦白講，我已經看出一條生路了！

第三場

〔傍晚，城中的公園，一個年輕人——楊森——穿著破爛，眼睛往上看正在公園上空弧形飛行的一架飛機。他從口袋中拿出一條繩子，小心翼翼地四周張望，當他走向一棵柳樹的時候，兩個妓女向他走來，其中一個已經老了，另一個是曾經去過沈蒂家的那位姪女。〕

年輕妓女　晚安，年輕人，要不要跟我來，小親親？

楊　森　可以，小姐們，如果你們能買些東西給我吃的話。

老妓女　你是個瘋子，是吧？（對年輕妓女）我們走吧，別跟他窮磨菇，他是個失業的飛行員。

年輕妓女　可是公園裡已經沒人了，而且就要下雨了。

老妓女　誰知道。

〔她們走開，楊森四周張望，又拿出繩子，往上丟往柳樹的樹枝，他露出困擾的樣子，兩個妓女很快又回來，但沒看見他。〕

年輕妓女　要下大雨了。

〔沈蒂走過來。〕

老妓女　瞧，那個妖精老了！她把你和你的家人害得真慘！

年輕妓女　不是她，是她的表哥，她收留我們，後來還幫我們付了蛋糕的錢，我對她沒什麼好批評的。

老妓女　可是我有！（大聲）哎喲，我們親愛的闊姊姊！她已經開了一家店，還來搶我們的男朋友呀！

沈　蒂　別血口噴人了，我正要去池塘旁的茶館呢。

年輕妓女　聽說你要和一個帶有三個小孩的鰥夫結婚，這可是真的？

沈　蒂　沒錯，我現在正要去那裡和他碰面。

楊　森　（不耐煩）走開，你們這些娘兒們！我想在這兒圖個安寧都不行嗎？

老妓女　你閉上你的鳥嘴！

〔兩個妓女退場。〕

楊　森　（在後面罵她們）禿鷹！（對著觀眾）你看連這麼偏僻的角落，她們都不放過獵食！即使在叢林裡，還在下著雨，她們也在到處找客人！

沈　蒂　（生氣）你怎麼罵她們？（她看到繩子）喔！

楊　森　你在瞪什麼？

沈　蒂　這條繩子幹什麼用的？

楊　森　你走吧，大姊，走吧！我沒錢，什麼都沒有，口袋半毛錢都沒有，即使我有錢，也不會想要嫖你，我會先買一杯水喝。

〔開始下雨。〕

沈　蒂　這條繩子幹什麼用的？你可別幹傻事！

楊　森　這干你屁事？走開！

沈　蒂　在下雨了。

楊　森　要不要到這樹下來躲雨？

沈　蒂　（在雨中站著，一動不動）不要。

楊　森　大姊，饒了我吧，沒有用的，別想跟我做生意，而且你也太醜了，一雙彎腿。

沈　蒂　你看錯了。

楊　森　別掀開！在下雨了，看老天份上，來樹下躲雨吧！

〔沈蒂慢慢走到樹下，坐了下來。〕

沈　蒂　你剛剛想幹嘛？

楊　森　你想知道嗎？我告訴你：我想擺脫你。（停頓）你知道當飛行員是怎麼回事嗎？

沈　蒂　我知道，我在茶館見過一些飛行員。

楊　森　不，你不知道，也許你見過幾個戴著皮製頭盔的傢伙，他們是些自負的白痴，對馬達聲一竅不通，對機器沒感覺，他們之所以能夠開飛機，那是因為他們賄賂了機場的管理員，你告訴其中隨便一個：「把飛機拉到兩千呎高，然後穿過雲層下降，然後手腕輕輕一扭，穩住飛機。」他會說：「合約上沒這個。」如果你開飛機，著陸的時候沒辦法乾淨俐落，你就是個蠢蛋，而不是飛行員，我是個飛行員，但也是個超級蠢蛋，我在北京飛行學校的時候，讀遍所有有關飛行的書，但是居然漏掉了一頁，上面說當局不再需要飛行員了，所以我就成了沒有飛機的飛行員，送郵件的飛行員，卻沒有郵件可送，我說了老半天這些，你是不會懂的。

沈　蒂　我想我懂。

楊　森　不，你絕對不會懂，你不可能懂的。

沈　蒂　（半笑半哭）小時候我們有一隻鶴，牠的一個翅膀壞掉了，牠很友善，不會在意我們開牠玩笑，牠每次跟在我們後面大步走，都會大叫要我們不要跑太快。可是秋天和春天來的時候，一大群鶴從我們村子上頭飛過，這時候牠就坐立不安了，所以我可以了解你的感受。（她開始哭。）

楊　森　別哭了。

沈　蒂　我偏要哭。

楊　森　再哭會傷身體的。

沈　蒂　我不哭了。

〔她用袖子擦眼淚，楊森靠著樹，身體不動，手伸向她的臉部。〕

楊　森　你連怎樣好好給自己擦臉都不懂。

〔他用手帕為她擦臉，停頓。〕

楊　森　如果你一定要待在這裡，我就不上吊了，可是你至少總得開口講話吧。

沈　蒂　我不知道要說什麼。

楊　森　你為什麼不讓我自殺，大姊？

沈　蒂　我害怕，我敢說你會想要自殺，是因為夜色顯得憂鬱的關係。

（對著觀眾）

在我們國內
不應該有憂鬱的夜晚，
河上的大橋
夜晚和早上之間的時辰
以及漫長的冬天：這些也都是危險的。
因為不管什麼樣的不幸
一點點就夠了
許多人就會因此丟棄
那無法忍受的生命。

楊　森　談談你自己吧。

沈　蒂　哪方面？我有一間小店。

楊　森　（揶揄）喔，你不是在賣春，你有一間店！

沈　蒂　（毅然地）我現在有一間店，可是以前我賣春。

楊　森　我猜想你的店是神明給你的禮物？

沈　蒂　是的。

楊　森　某一個晴朗的傍晚，他們出現，站在那裡，說：「這些錢拿去吧。」是這樣嗎？

沈　蒂　（輕聲笑）不是傍晚，是早上。

楊　森　你真有意思。

沈　蒂　（停頓一會兒）我會彈一點古箏，也會模仿別人，（她以低沈的聲音模仿大官說話）「好吧，考慮一下，我一定是把錢留在家裡了！」可是不久我就開店了，之後第一件事情就是把古箏丟開，然後我對自己說，我要像一條魚一樣悶聲不響，這不會有什麼不一樣的。

我說，我現在有錢了，

我自己走路，自己睡覺。

我說，整整一年

我都不要和男人有任何瓜葛。

楊　森　可是你現在要和人結婚了是嗎？就是池塘旁邊茶館裡的那個人？

〔沈蒂沈默不語。〕

楊　森　你對愛到底知道有多少？

沈　蒂　全部。

楊　森　你完全不懂，大姊，（停頓）也許你喜歡愛？

沈　蒂　不。

楊　森　（身體不動，伸手撫摸她的臉）舒服嗎？

沈　蒂　是的。

楊　森　我要說，你真容易滿足。好一個城鎮！

沈　蒂　你沒什麼朋友嗎？

楊　森　有許多，可是沒有人理會我一直沒有工作做，他們還扮鬼臉，好像我在抱怨不該抱怨的事情一樣，你應該也有朋友吧？

沈　蒂　（猶豫）我有一個表哥。

楊　森　要提防他。

沈　蒂　他只來過這裡一次，現在他早走了，而且再也不會回來了。你講話為什麼那麼絕望？人家說，講話不帶希望就表示也不帶善良。

楊　森　繼續說下去，不要讓聲音中斷。

沈　蒂　（熱切地）雖然到處都有不幸，好心的人還是很多。記得小時候，我背著一捆柴跌倒了，一個老人扶我起來，還給了我一毛錢，我常常想起這件事情，我特別想到有些人自己都沒得吃了，還會施捨東西給人。一般人大多喜歡讓人知道他所做的，他們更希望別人知道他們做得很好，但就是缺乏善心，做壞事其實很笨，但做好事卻很簡單，譬如唱一首歌、造一個機器或種一些稻，這些都是有善心的表現，像你就是個有善心的人。

楊　森　在你眼中看來，要有善心並不是很難。

沈　蒂　不難，我感覺到被雨水滴到了。

楊　森　哪裡？

沈　蒂　兩眼之間。

楊　森　靠近右眼還是左眼。

沈　蒂　靠近左眼。

楊　森　好了。（一會兒之後，想睡的樣子）你不再和男人有瓜葛了？

沈　蒂　（微笑）可是我的雙腿並沒有彎曲。

楊　森　也許沒有。

沈　蒂　絕對沒有。

楊　森　（疲倦，靠著樹）我已經兩天沒吃東西，一天沒喝水了，我很想愛你，卻沒有力量愛你。

沈　蒂　淋雨真棒。

〔賣水的老王出現，唱歌。〕

「賣水的人雨中之歌」

我在賣水，水，
我矗立在雨中。
為了這一點點水，
我不知吃盡多少苦頭。
我大聲喊：「買水呀！」
沒有人來買水，
乾透了，快死了，
趕快喝水，趕快付錢！
買水呀，你們這些狗！

喔，真希望這雨趕快停！
昨晚睡覺我又夢見
已經七年沒下雨了，
我一滴一滴施捨水，
喔，他們這樣大聲喊叫：「水！水！」
每一個來我這裡的人
我仔細看他們是否

我真的喜歡他們的臉孔，
每個人的舌頭都往外伸！

〔笑〕

現在大家的背都斜靠著
小小農作物同時
飲著雲層滴下來的奶汁
但從來不問：多少錢？
我大聲喊：「買水呀！」
沒有人來買水，
乾透了，快死了，
趕快喝水，趕快付錢！
買水呀，你們這些狗！

〔雨停了，沈蒂看到老王，跑過去。〕

沈　蒂　喔，老王，你回來啦？你的拐杖還留在我家裡。

老　王　謝謝你幫我保管！你還好吧，沈蒂？

沈　蒂　很好，我遇到一個既聰明又勇敢的人，我想跟你買杯水。

老　王　頭往後仰，嘴張開，要多少水就有多少水，那邊的那棵柳樹還在滴水呢。

沈　蒂

可是我要你的水，老王，
遠方帶來的水
這水讓你疲憊不堪
因為下雨了你的水一定不好賣。

我要買水給那邊那位先生。
他是個飛行員，
飛行員比一般人大膽，
他們與雲朵為伍！
無視於暴風的存在，
他穿越天空飛翔，
把友誼的信件
帶給遠方的朋友。

〔她付錢，拿著杯子跑向楊森。〕

沈 蒂 （回頭對老王叫，笑著）他睡著了，絕望、雨、還有我把他給累壞了。

第三場 A

〔下水道，老王棲息的地方，老王正在睡覺，下水道變成透明，眾神明出現在老王的夢中。〕

老　王　（快活地）我見過她了，大爺們！她還是老樣子。

神明甲　我們很高興她沒變。

老　王　她在戀愛了！我還看到了她的朋友，她現在可真的闊了。

神明甲　那真是好消息，我們希望這會給她帶來行善的推動力量。

老　王　那絕對！她一直盡其所能在行善。

神明甲　什麼樣的善？告訴我們，親愛的老王！

老　王　她對每一個人都說好話。

神明甲　（熱切地）是的，還有呢……？

老　王　任何人即使身上沒錢，到她的店裡都可以帶走一些煙草的。

神明甲　這聽起來不錯，還有沒有別的？

老　王　她收留過一家八口人。

神明甲　（得意地對著神明乙）八口人！（對著老王）也許還有別的？

老　王　下雨的時候她跟我買過一杯水。

神明甲　當然，這些都是小善行，這可以理解。

老　王　但是這也挺耗錢的，一家小店能提供的還是很有限。

神明甲　那當然，一個勤奮的園丁只要一小塊地就能創造奇蹟。

老　王　她正是如此！她每天早上都捐出米，我敢說這就耗去了她所賺的一半了。

神明甲　（有些失望）這沒什麼好挑剔的了，剛剛開始，這算差強人意了。

老　王　可是時機也不全然是好的，有一次她的店陷入困境，還必須找她的表哥來幫忙。

才剛剛找到一個可檔風雨的地方
一群烏從空中飛嘯而來
飛來爭奪這個地方
然後飢餓的狐狸跑來咬穿薄薄的牆
還有獨腳狼把小盤子打翻了。

總之，她再也無法自己處理事務了，但是大家都一致認定她是個好女孩，大家都叫她「郊區天使」，木匠林吐還有什麼好說的！

神明甲 此話何解？木匠林吐說她的壞話嗎？

老　王 喔，他只說店裡架子的錢沒有付清。

神明乙 你在說什麼？木匠的錢沒付？在沈蒂的店裡？她怎麼會幹這種事情？

老　王 我猜想她沒錢。

神明乙 欠錢就得還錢，沒有錢也要還，我們不允許不公平的事情發生，我們要先貫徹戒律的表面意義，然後是精紳。

老　王 但那是她的表哥幹的，大爺，不是她！

神明乙 那麼，就不要再讓她的表哥走進她的家門！

老　王 （喪氣）我知道，大爺。可是說句公道話，看在沈蒂的份上，她的表哥是一位相當受人尊敬的生意人，連警察也很看重他。

神明甲 當然，我們對這位表哥了解不多，實在也不能過份苛責他。我必須承認我對做生意完全外行，我不知道一般的慣例是怎樣，但是，生意── 是那麼必不可缺的嗎？這年頭每個人都在做生意！七善王有做過生意嗎？正直的孔子他賣魚嗎？做生意和誠實高尚的生活有關係嗎？

神明乙　（患重感冒）不管怎樣，這種事情絕不能再發生。（他轉身要走，另兩位神明也跟著轉身。）

神明丙　（最後轉身，困惑地）你一定要諒解我們今天講話的口氣，我們太累了，而且睡眠不足，老是為找晚上睡覺的地方傷腦筋！有錢人把我們推薦給窮人，可是窮人住的地方又太小。

眾神明　（離去，抱怨）軟弱，這些人們！優柔寡斷！太小了，太小了！有心，卻無力行動！至少，她應該看看這個……。

〔他們的聲音漸去漸遠，直到完全消失。〕

老　王　（叫他們）喔，請息怒，大爺們！不要一次要求太多！

第四場

〔沈蒂的煙草店門前的廣場，一家理髮店、一家地毯店，以及沈蒂的煙草店。早上，沈蒂店的門口，八口之家中的兩名份子，爺爺和弟媳婦，他們在等人。另有兩個人，一位是失業者，另一位是辛大太，也在等人。〕

弟媳婦　她昨晚沒回來。

辛太太　真是無法理解的行為！那位瘋狂表哥終於走了，女主人才能又多多少少給我們一些米，可是她昨晚竟然徹夜未歸，天曉得去了哪裡！

〔理髮店傳來叫鬧聲，老王蹣跚走出理髮店，肥胖的理髮匠師傅先生跟在後面，手上拿著一根彎曲的鐵棒。〕

師　傅　教訓你別再拿你的臭水來干擾我的客人！拿你的杯子給我滾蛋！

〔老王伸手去拿師傅手上的杯子，師傅專用鐵棒打他的手，老王痛得大叫。〕

師　傅　自作自受！給你一次教訓！（他氣呼呼的走回理髮店裡。）

失業者　（拾起杯子，遞給老王）你可以去警察局告他打你。

老　王　我的手痛死了。

失業者　是不是斷了？

老　王　不能動。

失業者　坐下來，在上面灑點水！

〔老王坐下〕

辛太太 你的水便宜，沒關係。

弟媳婦 大清早八點鐘在這裡也不能弄到尼龍布，她還沒回來，一定去玩樂去了，真不要臉！

辛太太 （憂慮地）她忘了我們！

〔沈蒂來到街上，手上拿著一盤米。〕

沈　蒂 （對著觀眾）我從未看過鎮上的早晨是什麼樣子，平常這個時候我都還躺在床上，頭上蒙著一條髒被子，害怕醒來。今天我走在送報的男孩中間，也走在刷走道的工人之間，還有那許多輛從鄉下運蔬菜進城的牛車。從楊森那裡走到這兒，走了好一段路，可是我卻走得輕鬆愉快，越走越愉快。我聽人說戀愛時走起路來都是輕飄飄的，好像走在雲端，但我覺得走在路上和走道上感覺真是愉快。我告訴你，早晨的時候，一排一排的房子看起來就像一堆一堆的圾垃，上頭有燈光照射著。天空是粉紅色的，因為還沒有塵埃，所以也是透明的。我告訴你，如果你不去戀愛，沒有看過早晨正在甦醒過來的四川，你就會覺得遺憾，這個時辰就像詩人所說的，好像安詳的老師傅深深吸一口新鮮空氣，伸手去拿工具準備上工。（對著正在等她的人們）早！米在這兒！（她攪動米，注意到老王）早，老王！我今天覺得有些昏昏然，在回家的路上，我不斷在商家的櫥窗裡看著我自己，我現在很想買條披肩，（遲疑一會兒）我想把自己打扮得漂亮些。（她很快走向地毯店。）

師　傅 （走出理髮店，對著觀眾）我很驚訝，因為我注意到沈蒂今天特別漂亮。她是對街那家煙草店的老闆，以前從未注意過她，剛才我仔細注視了她三分鐘，現在我覺得我已經愛上她了，好一個迷人的傢伙！（對老王）滾開，你這混帳的東西！（他走回店裡，沈蒂、老婦人以及她的丈夫走出地毯店，沈蒂披著一條披肩，老婦人的丈夫拿著一個鏡子。）

老婦人 很漂亮，而且不貴，因為底下有個小洞所以就賣便宜了。

沈　蒂 （看著老婦人身上的披肩）你這條綠色的也不錯。

老婦人 （微笑）只是這條沒有瑕疵。

沈　蒂 是啊，真可惜，太貴了我又買不起，我的小店收入不多，開銷卻又特別大。

老婦人 你花費不少在行善上面，但要小心，就說吧，每一盤米都要花錢的不是嗎？

沈　蒂 （試披有個小洞的披肩）事情就是這個樣子，我現在腦筋有些不清楚，我懷疑這個顏色是不是適合我？

老婦人 這個問題應該問男人。

沈　蒂 （轉向老闆）你覺得呢？

老　闆 何不問……

沈　蒂 （禮貌地）不，我在問你。

老　闆 （也禮貌地）這條披肩適合你，披的時候把不好看的那一面翻過去。

〔沈蒂付錢。〕

老婦人 如果你不喜歡，可以隨時拿回來換。（她把沈蒂拉到一旁）他有錢嗎？

沈　蒂 （笑）喔，沒有！

老婦人 那你怎麼付房租？

沈　蒂　房租？我已經整個忘了！

老婦人　我想也是，下禮拜一是月初，有些事情我想和你談一下，你知道，我和我丈夫認識你之後，對你的徵婚啟事覺得不是很可靠，一開始就決定要是結果不妙就伸手幫你，我們有一點積蓄，可以借你兩百大洋，只要用你煙草的存貨保證就可以，書面的借據當然就不需要了。

沈　蒂　你真的願意把錢借給像我這樣頭腦不清楚的人嗎？

老婦人　不瞞你說，要是你表哥就不會借—— 他頭腦精得很，可是我們願意借你，也不用擔心什麼。

老　闆　（走向他們）決定了嗎？

沈　蒂　我真希望神明們有聽到剛剛你太太講的話，馬先生，他們一直在找快樂的好人，你幫助我一定覺得快樂，我是為了愛才惹上麻煩的。

〔這對老夫婦互相對視而笑。〕

老　闆　錢在這裡。

〔他交給沈蒂一個信封，沈蒂接下，鞠躬，老婦人也跟著鞠躬，然後回去自己的店裡。〕

沈　蒂　（手上拿著信封，對老王）這個就是半年的房租！這是不是奇蹟？我的披肩好看嗎，老王？

老　王　你是為我在公園裡看到的那個傢伙而買的？

〔沈蒂點頭。〕

辛太太 也許你該看看他被打傷的手？也順便告訴他你多彩多姿的夜遊！

沈　蒂 （嚇一跳）你的手怎麼啦？

辛太太 理髮匠在眾目睽睽之下用鐵棒打傷的。

沈　蒂 （為自己的疏忽訝異）我怎麼會沒注意到！趕快去看醫生，要不然你的手會僵掉，以後不能幹活。真是何等不幸！趕快，起來！去，快去！

失業者 他不是該去看醫生，而是去找法官才對，他可以向理髮匠要求賠償，那小子有錢。

老　王 可能嗎？

辛太太 如果你的手斷了的話，斷了嗎？

老　王 應該是，已經腫起來了，也許可以弄到津貼？

辛太太 要有證人。

老　王 你們都瞧見了！你們可以作證嗎？

〔他環顧一下，失業者、爺爺、弟媳婦都靠牆坐著，正在吃東西，沒人理會他。〕

沈　蒂 （對辛太太）但你自己看到了！

辛太太 我不想和警察有任何瓜葛。

沈　蒂 （對弟媳婦）你呢？

弟媳婦 我？我沒看到！

辛太太 你絕對有看到！我看到你在看！可是你害怕，因為理髮匠會報復。

沈　蒂 （對爺爺）我敢說你會作證！

弟媳婦 他的證詞不會被採納，因為他的腦筋痴呆。

沈　蒂 （對失業者）這是一件關係到終生津貼的事情。

失業者 我已因乞討被逮捕了兩次，我的證詞只有對他有害。

沈　蒂 （不太相信）這麼說來你們沒有人願意作證了？他的手在光天化日下被打斷，你們都當場看到了，卻沒有人願意出來講話！

（生氣）

不快樂的人們！

你的兄弟被攻擊而你竟閉著眼睛！

他被打了大聲哀號而你竟沈默不語？

野獸出來尋覓獵物而你卻說：

他為我們犧牲因為我們高興他這樣做。

這是什麼城市啊？你們是哪類人啊？

當不公正出現時這個城市就應該有反叛。

如果沒有反叛，那這個城市最好在日落前被一把火燒掉！

老王，既然這些人都不願意為你作證，我來，我說我是證人。

辛太太 這會成為偽證。

老　王 我不知道我能否接受，也許可以。（看著他的手，憂慮）你看這手是不是很腫？好像消腫了是不是？

失業者 （確定地）不，絕對沒有消腫。

老　王 沒有嗎？我看好像更腫了，也許連整個手腕都斷了！我應該趕快去找法官。

〔老王小心翼翼扶著手並且不斷看著，跑著離去，辛太太跑進理髮店。〕

失業者 她要去站在理髮匠那一邊了。

弟媳婦 我們無法改變這個世界。

沈　蒂 （沮喪）我不想責備你們，我只是怕，不，我不想責備，你們都走開吧！

〔失業者、弟媳婦，以及爺爺等一邊吃著喝著一邊離去。〕

沈　蒂　（對著觀眾）
他們沒有話可說了，
誰收留他們，他們就留在那裡，
誰趕他們走
他們很快就走，
只有食物的香味才會引起他們注意。

〔一位老女人跑著走過來。〕

老女人　（喘著氣）你是沈蒂小姐嗎？我的兒子已經把一切都告訴我了，我是楊森的母親楊太太，他現在有一個機會可以成為飛行員。今天早上，剛才而已，北京來了一封信，從航空郵件服務中心的經理那裡來的。

沈　蒂　他又可以飛行了嗎？喔，楊太太！

楊太太　可是這個職位得花上好一筆錢，五百塊大洋。

沈　蒂　這可不是一筆小數目，但是不能讓錢的問題妨礙這樣的事情，不管怎麼，我還有這家店！

楊太太　真希望你能幫點什麼的！

沈　蒂　（擁抱她）我會的！

楊太太　你會給一個有才幹的年輕人機會？

沈　蒂　我們怎能阻撓一個人去成為有用之材？（停頓一下）只是這間店還不夠，我這裡有兩百塊大洋，還是剛剛才借來的，你先拿去吧，我會賣掉煙草的存貨來償還。（她把老婦人的錢交給楊太太。）

楊太太　喔，沈蒂小姐，你的幫忙來得真是時候！他們以前都叫他做

四川的死飛行員，都一致認定他絕不可能再有機會飛行了！

沈　蒂　可是我們還差三百塊大洋，我們得想辦法，楊太太，（慢慢地）我知道有個人可以幫我們這個忙，他以前幫過我，我實在很不願意再去找他，他這個人狡猾不好惹，希望這是最後一次了。不管怎樣，飛行員一定得飛，這是最明顯不過了。

〔遠處傳來引擎聲。〕

楊太太　真希望你說的那個人真能弄到錢！瞧，那是早班的郵件飛機，去北京的！

沈　蒂　（剛毅地）揮手，楊太太！我敢說那飛行員一定會看到我們！（她揮動她的披肩）趕快揮手！

楊太太　（揮手）你認識上面在飛的飛行員嗎？

沈　蒂　不認識，可是我認識即將要飛的那一位，他曾經放棄希望，可是他現在就快要飛了，楊太太，他就要脫離困境，超越在我們每個人之上了！（對著觀眾）

楊森，我的愛人，
與白雲為伍！
衝破暴風雨
穿透天空
帶給遠方朋友
友誼的信件。

第四場 A

〔在簾幕前面，沈蒂出現，手上拿著蕭大的西裝和面具，她唱：〕

「神明與好人的不設防之歌」

在我們的國家裡
有用的人需要運氣
只要能夠找到有力的幫忙者
他就能夠證明自己有用。
好人無法幫助自己
神明也是無能為力。
為什麼神明沒有地雷、大砲
戰艦、轟炸機，以及坦克車呢？
為什麼不毀掉壞人拯救好人呢？
我們是不是沒有必要感恩？

〔她穿上蕭大的西裝，學他的樣子走幾步路。〕

好人
在我們的國家無法永遠保持做好人。
盤子空了，晚餐時就爭吵，
哎，神明的戒律
面對匱乏時一無用處。
神明為什麼不出現在市場上
微笑著給人們分配食物？
讓每個人任意吃和喝

然後對自己的兄弟好而有愛心？

〔她戴上蕭大的面具，現在以他的聲音唱歌。〕

為了得到一頓晚餐
你必須像開創帝國那樣努力。
不踐踏十二個人
你就無法幫助一個窮人。
那麼神明們在天上為什麼不說話
說這個世界之所以好是因為有好人？
為什麼他們不帶著炸彈站在好人旁邊
開砲讓一切一了百了？

第五場

〔煙草店，蕭大坐在櫃台後面看報紙。他一點都沒留意到辛太太在旁邊，她正一邊清理東西，一邊說話。〕

辛太太 要是謠言在這一帶繼續再散播下去，像這樣的一家小店遲早會垮的，相信我，你是個正人君子，該是正視沈蒂和黃街那位楊森兩人之間曖昧關係的適當時機了，別忘了隔壁理髮店的師傅先生，他有十二棟房子，才一個太太，太太老了，昨天我看到他對沈蒂好像是挺有意思的，我看他是很認真的，他還打聽她的經濟狀況，這很明顯，我敢說他是真的有那個意思了。

〔她看蕭大沒有答話，就逕自帶著桶子出去了。〕

楊　森 （從外面）這是沈蒂的店嗎？

辛太太的聲音 是啊，沒錯，可是今天她的表哥在這兒。

〔蕭大邁著沈蒂的輕盈腳步，跑向鏡子，她注意到鏡子裡有些不對，開始整理頭髮，然後輕輕笑著轉開。楊森進來，辛太太好奇地跟著進來，從他身旁經過，然後進入後面的房間。〕

楊　森 我是楊森，（向蕭大鞠躬）沈蒂在嗎？

蕭　大 不，她不在。

楊　森 我猜你知道我和她的關係？（他開始環視店裡一切）真正活生生的店！我一直以為她在吹牛，（他看看一些小盒子及陶器罐子，覺得很滿意）老兄，我又要去飛行了！（他拿了一支雪茄，蕭大為他點火）你認為我們能夠從這家店再擠出三百塊大洋嗎？

蕭　大　請問你想立刻賣掉這家店嗎？

楊　森　如果賣了，我們能馬上拿到三百塊大洋現金嗎？（蕭大搖頭）也真難為她了，馬上就拿出了兩百塊大洋，但是還差三百塊大洋，還是沒什麼用。

蕭　大　也許她答應你答應得太輕率了，那可真得賣了這家店才行，俗話說，太急的風會吹垮鷹架。

楊　森　我需要這筆錢很急，如果不能馬上拿到就不要了，而且讓你等的也不是這個女孩而已，你總是等這個或等那個的，我的意思你懂了沒有？

蕭　大　我懂。

楊　森　啊哈。

蕭　大　我可不可以知道這五百塊大洋做什麼用的？

楊　森　當然可以，這我就要直說了，北京機場的管理員是我在飛行學校時候的一個朋友，只要我能弄到五百塊大洋，他就能幫我弄到那個職位。

蕭　大　要這樣一筆錢是不是太貴了點？

楊　森　不會，他要叫他目前的一個飛行員走路，因為那個傢伙有過失，他想用另一個人，可是這個人有許多家人要養，這樣講你可以懂的，我們私底下講這件事，不要讓沈蒂知道。

蕭　大　也許，還有一件事——那位管理員可不會下個月又要叫你走路吧？

楊　森　不會，我在工作上絕不會犯錯，我失業太久了。

蕭　大　（點頭）餓狗拉車總是特別起勁。（他仔細看他）你的責任很重大，楊森先生，你要我表妹放棄她這小小的資產，離開這鎮上所有的朋友，然後把她整個命運都交到你手中，我猜你預備和她結婚是吧？

楊　森　正有此意。

蕭　大　為了區區幾百塊大洋而賣掉這家店是不是太可惜了一點？如果要馬上賣掉，那是真不划算的，你手上的那兩百塊大洋本來是要用來預付半年的房租的，你有沒有想過也一起來賣煙草？

楊　森　我來賣煙草？堂堂飛行員的楊森被人家看到站在櫃台後面：「您要烈的還是淡一點的雪茄，大爺？」這不是楊森幹的事情，至少不是在這個世紀！

蕭　大　恕我冒昧這樣問，搞飛行賺錢嗎？

楊　森　（從口袋裡拿出一封信）先生，我一個月可以拿兩百五十塊大洋！你自己看這封信，上面貼著郵票，還蓋有郵戳，北京。

蕭　大　兩百五十塊大洋？那真不少。

楊　森　你以為我飛行是為了好玩？

蕭　大　這個職位似乎相當不錯，楊森先生，我的表妹委託我幫你去弄到這個職位，這對你是那麼的重要，從她的觀點來看，我沒什麼好理由可以反對她的心意，她有權利去體驗愛情的喜悅，我預備把這裡的一切都變賣，房東梅珠太太來了，我要她給我一些建議怎麼變賣。

房東太太　（進來）你好，蕭大先生，是不是後天該繳房租了吧？

蕭　大　梅珠太太，情況有了變化，我表妹可能不想開店了，她預備要結婚，她的未婚夫（他介紹楊森）楊森先生要帶她一塊上北京去過新的生活，這些煙草如果有好價錢，我就賣了。

房東太太　你需要多少錢？

楊　森　三百塊大洋。

蕭　大　（很快）不，五百！

房東太太　（對楊森）也許我可以幫你忙，你的煙草值多少錢？

蕭　大　我表妹付了一千塊大洋，只賣出一些而已。

房東太太　一千塊大洋！她被敲竹槓啦，就這麼說定，整間店我付你

三百塊大洋，你後天搬出去。

楊　森　就這麼辦，絕對可以，老兄！

蕭　大　太少了。

楊　森　夠了！

蕭　大　必須五百塊大洋才行。

楊　森　為什麼？

蕭　大　（對房東太太）我和我表妹的未婚夫商議一下，（把楊森拉到一旁）昨天給你的那兩百塊大洋，是用店裡的煙草作擔保跟對面的老夫婦借來的。

楊　森　有立書面契約嗎？

蕭　大　沒有。

楊　森　（對房東太太）三百塊大洋可以。

房東太太　可是我要知道這店有沒有負債。

楊　森　你回答！

蕭　大　這店沒有負債。

楊　森　什麼時候可以拿到三百塊大洋？

房東太太　後天，你們還可以考慮考慮，你們要是不要賣這麼急，價錢可以高一點，我願意付三百塊大洋是因為這對年輕人的愛情，我想樂觀其成。（退場）

楊　森　（在她後面叫）就這麼定了！小盒子、罐子、袋子，就這樣三百塊大洋打發了，煩惱也解除了。（對蕭大）也許後天之前我們還可以找到別人賣更高的價錢？

蕭　大　這麼短的時間不可能，除了梅珠太太那三百塊大洋之外，我們一文不名，路上的旅費，以及前面幾個禮拜的生活，你身上還有錢負擔這些嗎？

楊　森　當然。

蕭　大　有多少？

楊　森　我會想辦法去弄，大不了用偷的！

蕭　大　喔，原來如此，這種小錢也需要用想辦法的？

楊　森　你也管太多了，老兄，我會有辦法去北京的。

蕭　大　兩個人一起會很花錢。

楊　森　兩個人？我不讓女孩跟去，開始的時候，她會是個大累贅。

蕭　大　原來如此。

楊　森　幹嘛那樣看我？好像我是個漏油桶子似的，你應該盡力把事情料理好。

蕭　大　我表妹要靠什麼過活？

楊　森　你不能幫她一點忙嗎？

蕭　大　我會的，（停頓）楊森先生，我希望你把那兩百塊大洋交給 我，除非你能讓我看到你有兩張到北京去的車票，否則這筆錢就扣在我這兒。

楊　森　我的老兄，我希望你只管你自己的事情就好。

蕭　大　沈蒂小姐……。

楊　森　把這女孩交給我就好。

蕭　大　……可能不想賣掉這家店，要是她知道……。

楊　森　她會的，即使她知道。

蕭　大　你不怕我干預嗎？

楊　森　我親愛的先生！

蕭　大　你好像忘了她也是人，她是有感覺的。

楊　森　（高興）有許多人對女人的看法，以及對理性勸導可能產生的作用，在我看來實在很不可思議，你聽說過愛情的力量嗎？肌膚之親？你要和她談理性？她根本不懂什麼叫做理性！再說，這可憐的傢伙也把自己糟蹋夠了，我只不過輕輕拍一下她的肩膀說：「跟我來。」她就像聽到鈴聲，忘了自己的母親了。

蕭　大　（痛苦地）楊森先生！

楊　森　老兄先生！

蕭　大　我表妹愛上你是因為……。

楊　森　是不是該說因為我摸了她的胸脯？你要把事情好好想清楚！（他又拿了一支雪茄，並放了一些在口袋，最後乾脆拿了一整盒夾在腋下）不要什麼都不給她，我們會結婚的，她會把三百塊大洋帶來，或者你帶來也行，她或你，誰帶來都可以！（退場）

辛太太　（從後面房間伸出頭來）好像不太對勁，整條黃街的人都知道他是真吃定這女孩了。

蕭　大　（大喊）這家店完了！他根本不愛她！我完了！（像關在籠裡的野獸團團轉，反覆叫著「這家店完了！」，然後突然停下來，對辛太太說話）辛太太，你窮人家出身，我也是，我們那麼卑賤嗎？不，我們的心腸不夠硬嗎？不，我要掐住你的喉，直到你從我這兒偷的乳酪都吐了出來。你知道，時機真壞，這個鎮活像個地獄，但是我們會漸漸掙脫出來的，只不過壞運道總會降臨在我們某些人身上：她戀愛了。這就夠了，她也跟著完了，只要有一項弱點，你就完了。你無能掙脫所有的弱點，特別是最要命的一個：愛？愛是絕對不可能的，太貴了！可是，告訴我，你能在生活中躲得掉這個嗎？這是個什麼樣的世界呀？

愛撫變成勒殺，
愛的嘆息變成害怕的叫喊，
為什麼禿鷹老在那上面盤旋？
一個女孩正要會見她的愛人。

辛太太　我看我還是趕快走，去把理髮匠找來，你和他好好談一下，他是個有名望的人，他很適合你的表妹。

〔她不等回答就逕自離去了，蕭大再度團團轉，直到師傅先生進來，辛太太跟在後面，但師傅跟她做手勢，要她退後。〕

蕭　大　（急著趨向他）我親愛的先生，我聽說你曾表示過對我表妹有意思，我現在也管不了禮節和含蓄的問題，沈蒂小姐目前的處境很危險。

師　傅　喔！

蕭　大　幾個鐘頭之前她還是她自己店的主人，現在卻變成只比乞丐好一點點而已。師傅先生，這家店完了。

師　傅　蕭大先生，沈蒂的魅力不在於她的店好，而是在於她的心地好，這一帶的人們給她取的外號就說明了這個，他們稱她為「郊區天使」！

蕭　大　我親愛的先生，她的好心地已經讓她在一天之內足足損失了兩百塊大洋，我們要想辦法阻止。

師　傅　容我表達我不同的看法，我們要敞開善良的大門，喜歡行善是這位年輕小姐的本性，每天早晨我看她拿東西給四個人吃，很覺感動，這說明什麼呢？為什麼她不拿東西給四百個人吃呢？我還聽說她絞盡腦汁想怎樣去收容一些無家可歸的人，我那牛棚後頭有幾個小房間，可隨時供她差遣使用。我聽了許多這一類有關她的善行，不勝枚舉……。蕭大先生，我真希望沈蒂小姐願意接納過去幾天我所想到的這些個主意，不知尊意如何？

蕭　大　師傅先生，她會很樂意聆聽您的高見的。

〔老王和警察進來，師傅先生轉頭看架上的東西。〕

老　王　沈蒂在嗎？

蕭　大　不在。

老　王　我是老王，賣水的人，我猜你就是蕭大先生？

蕭　大　在下正是，你好，老王。

老　王　我是沈蒂的朋友。

蕭　大　你是她的老朋友，我知道。

老　王　（對警察）你看到了吧？（對蕭大）我為了我的手而來。

警　察　毫無疑問，他的手斷了。

蕭　大　（很快）我看你需要一條吊帶。（他從後面房間拿出一條披肩，丟給老王。）

老　王　那是她新買的披肩呀。

蕭　大　她不用了。

老　王　那是她買來取悅某人的。

蕭　大　事情有了變卦，她不再需要了。

老　王　（用披肩弄成吊帶把手懸住）她是我唯一的證人。

警　察　理髮匠師傅用鐵棒子打這位賣水的人的時候，聽說你表妹看到了，你知道這件事吧？

蕭　大　我只知道事情發生時我表妹並不在場。

老　王　這是誤會！我們等沈蒂回來就會真相大白了，她可以作證，她上哪兒去了？

蕭　大　（嚴肅地）王先生，你說你是我表妹的朋友，我表妹現在麻煩已經夠多了，四面八方都要壓榨她，她已經所剩無幾了，我相信你現在不會願意要她出來說假話，弄得更狼狽吧！

老　王　（困惑地）是她勸我去找法官的。

蕭　大　法官會醫你手上的傷嗎？（師傅先生轉過頭來）王先生，我有一個原則，就是絕不插手干預朋友之間的糾紛。（蕭大向師傅先生鞠躬，師傅先生回敬。）

老　王　（拿下手上的披肩，放回去，傷心地）我了解。

警　察　我想我可以走了，你去找一個高尚的人——你如果想騙人，那就錯了。下次要告人的時候，最好小心一點，要不是師傅先生慈悲為懷，你可能就要因為誣告而坐牢，你現在滾吧。（退場）

蕭　大　發生這事，請勿見怪。

師　傅　不會的，那裡。（急切地）和「某人」（指著披肩）的那檔事是已經結束了吧？完完全全的結束了？

蕭　大　完全結束，她已經把他看穿了，當然，要她整個恢復過來，恐怕還得等上一陣吧。

師　傅　我們行事應該謹慎，小心為是。

蕭　大　還有一些新的創傷。

師　傅　她應該到鄉下去。

蕭　大　去住幾個禮拜，不過，在那之前她得和一個她信得過的人好好談一下。

師　傅　到一家小而好的餐館吃頓小小的晚餐。

蕭　大　以小心謹慎的方式進行，我得趕快通知我表妹，她會通達情理的，她現在很擔心她的這家店，她一直認為這是神明給她的禮物，請稍候片刻。（退入後面房間。）

辛太太　（探頭進來）我該恭喜你了吧？

師　傅　辛太太，你今天可以讓沈蒂小姐收留的客人知道，說我可以讓他們使用我那牛棚後面的幾個小房間。

〔她點頭，露齒而笑。〕

師　傅　（站起來，對著觀眾）先生女士們，你們覺得我這個人怎麼樣？

誰可以比我做得更多？誰可以比我更不自私？更有遠見？一頓小小的晚餐！許多人對這種事情可能會產生粗俗愚蠢的想法，但這不會發生，不會的，沒有人會去碰她，絕對不會，即使偶而一起吃飯也不會。只有觀念能夠互相溝通，兩個人會因為對桌上的花朵看法一致而互相了解，比如說白色的菊花。（他記下筆記）不，我們不能因為別人不幸就去加以剝削，去加以佔便宜，諒解和協助才是必要的，但不能出聲，單單一個眼神就夠了，一個眼神就可以帶來許多的意義。

辛太太 每一件事都如你的意，師傅先生？

師　傅 喔，都如我的意！這個地區可能會有一些改變，這裡的大門已經為某人敞開，企圖染指這家店的陰謀會被破壞，有些人膽敢傷害本鎮最貞節女孩的名譽，我就和他們沒完沒了，你對那個楊森了解有多少？

辛太太 他不但是最髒，而且也最懶……。

師　傅 他什麼都不是，他不存在，他會不見，辛太太。（楊森進來。）

楊　森 這裡發生什麼事？

辛太太 師傅先生，要我叫蕭大先生嗎？他不會喜歡陌生人在他店裡閒蕩的。

師　傅 沈蒂小姐和蕭大先生正在商議重要的事情，不要打擾他們。

楊　森 什麼？她在這裡？我居然沒看到她進來！他們在商議什麼事情？我必須進去參與！

師　傅 （阻擋他進入後面房間）要有耐性，我親愛的先生，我想我知道你是誰，請留神我和沈蒂正準備要宣佈訂婚。

楊　森 什麼？

辛太太 你吃驚了，是吧？

〔楊森正和理髮匠拉扯要進入後面房間時，沈蒂走了出來。〕

師　傅　對不起，沈蒂小姐，也許你可以解釋一下……。

楊　森　到底怎麼回事，沈蒂？你瘋了嗎？

沈　蒂　（喘著氣）楊森，我表哥和師傅先生達成一項協議：關於如何去幫助這一帶的人，我要採納師傅先生的意見。（停一下）我的表哥不要我們在一起。

楊　森　你同意了？

沈　蒂　是的。

〔停頓一下。〕

楊　森　他們是不是告訴你，說我是壞人。

〔沈蒂不說話。〕

楊　森　也許我真的是壞人，沈蒂，所以我才需要你，我低賤，沒有 錢，沒有儀態，但我有進取心，他們要把你推入不幸，沈蒂，（他走向她並壓低聲音）你看看他！你沒有眼睛看嗎？（把一隻手放在她肩膀上）可憐的人，他們要你做什麼？嫁個好人家！我一不在，他們就打算要把你犧牲掉，不要否認，要不是我，你恐怕已經跟他走了！

沈　蒂　是的。

楊　森　一個你不愛的人。

沈　蒂　是的。

楊　森　你忘了我們的約定了嗎？那場大雨也忘了嗎？

沈　蒂　沒忘。

楊　森　你怎樣把我從樹上救下來的？你怎樣買水給我喝的？你怎樣答應給我那筆錢好讓我再飛行的？

沈　蒂　（顫抖著）你要我怎麼樣？

楊　森　我要你和我一塊走。

沈　蒂　師傅先生，原諒我，我要和楊森一起走。

楊　森　我們是情人，你知道，（他拉著她走向門口）店的鑰匙在哪裡？（他從她口袋拿出鑰匙，交給辛太太），走的時候記得把它留在門外，走吧，沈蒂。

師　傅　這簡直是強暴！（向後面大叫）蕭大先生！

楊　森　告訴他不要在這裡叫那麼大聲。

沈　蒂　請不要叫我表哥，師傅先生，他不同意我，我知道，但他錯了，我可以感覺得到。（對著觀眾）

我要和我愛的人一起走
我不要計較一切利益得失
我不要考慮這是否明智之舉
我要和我愛的人一起走。

楊　森　這就對了。（全退場）

第五場A

〔簾幕前，沈蒂穿著結婚禮服，正準備要去出席自己的婚禮，她轉向觀眾。〕

沈　蒂　我剛經歷一次極不尋常的經驗，步出房門的時候，我覺得很愉快，心裡充滿期待。地毯店老闆的太太站在大街上，全身顫抖著，她還含著眼淚祝福我，並且希望我不要介意，因為她無法全然信得過我表哥，也信不過楊森，這真是遺憾。她走了之後，我必須坐下來，我被我自己的舉止嚇到了，我的情感澎湃不已，竟不顧一切委身給了楊森，我無法抗拒他的聲音和他的愛撫，他對蕭大說的那些狠話對沈蒂竟然無濟於事，躺在他懷抱裡的時候，我這樣想：神明也希望我對自己行些善事。

不要別人毀滅，也不要自己毀滅，
要別人幸福，也要自己幸福，
這就是行善了。

我怎麼忘得了那對和善的老夫婦呢？楊森就像一場小颶風，吹掉我的店和我所有的朋友，目標直指向北京，不過他還不壞，他愛我，只要我和他在一起，他就不會幹壞事，別人怎麼說他都無所謂，他有野心，充滿自信，但同時也很冷酷。我告訴他那對老夫婦付不出稅金時，他就會了解一切了，他寧可到水泥廠做工也不願意為了飛行而去幹壞勾當，當然他對飛行懷有極大的熱情，我想帶他向善，但不知道力量夠不夠？現在我要去出席自己的婚禮了，我擺盪在恐懼和喜悅之間。（她快速離去。）

第六場

〔郊區一家廉價餐廳的邊房，婚禮上一個服務生正在為客人倒酒，沈蒂旁邊是爺爺、弟媳婦、姪女、辛太太，以及失業者，角落上站著一位牧師，台下楊森正在和他母親說話，他穿一件晚宴外套。〕

楊　森　事情有些不對勁，媽媽，她剛才不經意告訴我說她不想為了我把店賣掉，有人宣稱店是他們的，因為他們借給了她兩百塊大洋，這筆錢她已經給了你，但她表哥說他們並沒有立任何書面契約。

楊太太　你對她怎麼說？顯然你現在不能和她結婚。

楊　森　現在和她談這些事情沒什麼用，她是個死腦筋，我已經派人去找她表哥來。

楊太太　可是她表哥想把她嫁給理髮匠。

楊　森　我已經把這件事解決掉了，那個理髮匠還為此受盡了屈辱，她表哥不久就會了解要是我不還出那兩百塊大洋，債權人就要接收那家店，店就完了，可是如果我沒拿到那三百塊大洋，我的職位也完了。

楊太太　我到餐廳外面去找他，你去陪你的新娘，現在，楊森！

沈　蒂　（倒酒，對著觀眾）我沒有看錯他，我在他臉上沒看到一絲失望的痕跡，放棄飛行對他而言打擊一定很大，可是他現在看起來還蠻愉快的，我很愛他。（她和楊森招手）楊森，你還沒和新娘敬酒喔！

楊　森　要敬什麼酒？

沈　蒂　為未來敬酒。

〔他們喝酒。〕

楊　森　希望以後新郎的晚禮服不必再用借的！

沈　蒂　希望新娘的衣服時時被雨淋濕。

楊　森　心想事成！

沈　蒂　很快就要實現了！

楊太太　（要出去時，對辛太太）我對我的兒子很滿意，我常常跟他說他要娶誰我都不會有意見，他是個經過訓練的機械師，也是個訓練有素的飛行員，你知道他現在跟我怎麼說？他說：「我為愛結婚，媽媽。」「金錢不是一切。」好一個有愛情基礎的結合！（對弟媳婦）事情總得發生一次的，不是嗎？可是這卻難為做母親的了，真是難為！（回頭對牧師喊叫）典禮不能太短，就像買東西講價時一樣，盡量把時間拖長一點，如果能這樣，那就會夠隆重的了。（對沈蒂）我們還是要再稍為拖延一會兒，親愛的，我們最看重的一位客人還沒到，（對其他客人）對不起，借過。（退場）

弟媳婦　只要有酒喝，我們會很有耐性的。

失業者　我們不會有什麼損失的。

楊　森　（在客人面前，大聲而帶開玩笑的口吻）在娶你進門之前，我恐怕得給你作個小小的測驗，當然，這麼寒酸的婚禮這似乎不太有必要，（對著客人）可是我不知道我要的是個什麼樣的太太，我很擔心這個，（對沈蒂）譬如，你能否用三片茶葉泡五杯茶？

沈　蒂　不能。

楊　森　我知道我沒茶可喝了，另一題，你有沒有辦法睡在像牧師在讀的那本書那麼小的裝稻草的布袋上面？

沈　蒂　和別人嗎？

楊　森　自己一個人。

沈　蒂　這樣的話，不能。

楊　森　娶這樣的太太真是叫人吃驚。

〔客人都在笑，楊太太從門口進來，走到沈蒂背後，聳一下肩，告訴楊森沒有他們正在等的客人的蹤影。〕

楊太太　（對牧師，他正亮錶給她看）不要急，再等幾分鐘，大家都在喝酒抽煙，看樣子並不急。（她在客人旁邊坐下來。）

沈　蒂　我們要不要談談怎麼安排事情？

楊太太　喔，拜託，不要再談店的事情，在典禮上還要談店的事，就有點不識大體了，你不覺得嗎？

〔大門的門鈴響了，大家看過去，但沒有人進來。〕

沈　蒂　你母親在等誰，楊森？

楊　森　你會意想不到，對了，你的表哥蕭大還好吧？我和他處得不錯，人很靈敏！腦筋很好！你怎麼不說話呢？

沈　蒂　我不知道，我不想去想他。

楊　森　為什麼？

沈　蒂　因為你不該和他處得好，你如果愛我，就不可能愛他。

楊　森　那麼我們希望有三個魔鬼來騷擾他：霧鬼、引擎搗蛋鬼，以及油箱掏空鬼！喝酒吧，你這頑固的女孩！（他迫使她喝酒。）

弟媳婦　（對辛太太）這裡事情有點不對勁。

辛太太　你想會怎麼樣？

牧　師　（堅決地走向楊太太，手上拿著一隻錶）我非走不可了，我還有另外一場婚禮要去，明天一早還有個葬禮喔。

楊太太　你以為我喜歡這樣拖延嗎？我們原先還希望一壺酒就夠了，現在搞成這個樣子！（大聲對沈蒂）我親愛的沈蒂，我真不懂你表哥在這節骨眼會跑去哪裡呢？

沈　蒂　我表哥？

楊太太　是的，沒錯，親愛的，我們一直在等的就是他！我這老古董總以為和新娘這麼親的一位親戚應該會來參加婚禮的。

沈　蒂　喔，楊森，是不是為了那三百塊大洋？

楊　森　（不看她）你沒聽到嗎？她是個老古董，好吧，算我多情，我們再等他十五分鐘，如果再不來，那恐怕是真的被那三個魔鬼給絆住了。

楊太太　我猜你們大概都已經知道我兒子就要去當郵件飛機的飛行員，我很高興，這年頭有錢賺就要好好去賺。

弟媳婦　那要去北京囉，是嗎？

楊太太　沒錯，北京。

沈　蒂　你應該告訴你母親，我們不去北京了。

楊　森　你表哥會告訴她，如果他同意你這樣做的話，至於我們之間，我不同意。

沈　蒂　（吃驚）楊森！

楊　森　我真討厭四川，什麼鬼地方！每當我眼睛半閉的時候，你知道他們這些人看起像什麼嗎？像馬！他們踏步前進，脖子拉得高高的，他們上面在喧鬧什麼？怎麼搞的？再也沒有人要他們了嗎？什麼，他們的時間已經到了？讓他們在這個馬鎮自己把自己咬死為止！喔，離開這裡吧！

沈　蒂　可是我已經答應那對老夫婦要還他們錢。

楊　森　是的，你說過了，自從你幹了那樁蠢事以後，幸虧你表哥來了，喝酒吧，事情讓我們來處理，我們會解決的。

沈　蒂　（害怕）但是我表哥不能來。

楊　森　怎麼說呢？

沈　蒂　他就是不能來。

楊　森　你要怎麼計劃我們的未來？告訴我。

沈　蒂　那兩百塊大洋想必還在你身上，我們明天把錢還了，煙草留著，那值很多錢，既然我們付不出那半年的房租，我們就一起到水泥廠門口賣煙草。

楊　森　不要提這個！拜託不要提這個了，大姊！你要我站在街上賣煙草給水泥工人，我，楊森，飛行員！我寧可一個晚上把那兩百塊大洋花掉！你表哥了解我，我已經和他安排好怎樣用這筆錢，他會把三百塊大洋帶到婚禮現場來。

沈　蒂　我表哥不會來。

楊　森　但我相信他不至於會不來。

沈　蒂　有我在的地方他就不會出現。

楊　森　好神秘！

沈　蒂　楊森，你必須了解一件事情:他不是你的朋友，愛你的人是我，他也不是我朋友的朋友，他同意你拿那對老夫婦的兩百塊大洋時，他只想到你在北京的職位，但是他今天是不會把三百塊大洋帶來婚禮現場的。

楊　森　為什麼不會？

沈　蒂　（仔細看著他）他說你只買一張到北京的車票。

楊　森　沒錯，那是昨天的事情，你看，今天不一樣了！（他從胸前口袋抽出半截的兩張紙）不要讓老太婆看到，這是兩張到北京的車票，一張給你，一張給我，你還是認為你表哥反對我們結婚嗎？

沈　蒂　不會，你那個職位是不錯，可是我的店卻要沒了。

楊　森　為了你，我已經賣掉了家具。

沈　蒂　不要去了！不要給我看那兩張車票！我很怕就這樣跟你去了，我無法給你那三百塊大洋，楊森，還有那對老夫婦怎麼辦？

楊　森　我呢？我怎麼辦？（停頓）再喝酒吧！你是個細心的人嗎？我

不要一個細心的太太，如果我喝酒了，我就會想要再飛，你呢，你如果喝酒了，你可能就會了解我了。

沈　蒂　別以為我不了解你，你想要飛，我卻無法幫你忙。

楊　森　「這裡有一架飛機，親愛的，只可惜少了一個翅膀！」

沈　蒂　楊森，我們不能問心無愧的去接北京那個職位，這就是為什麼我一定要拿回給你的那兩百塊大洋的理由，現在還給我，楊森！

楊　森　「現在還給我，楊森！」你到底在胡扯些什麼？你是我太太嗎？或者不是？你在背叛我，你不覺得嗎？還好事情並不是由你作決定，所有事情早就安排好了。

楊太太　（冷冷的）楊森，你確定新娘的表哥一定會來？你看他現在還不來，可見一定不是很贊成這個婚姻。

楊　森　媽媽，你想到哪裡去了？我和他是很要好的朋友！我要把大門打開，讓他來當他的好朋友楊森的最佳伴郎時，一走進來 就看見我們。（他走過去，用腳把大門踢開，然後搖晃地走 回來，他喝太多了，他坐到沈蒂旁邊）我們還在等，你的表 哥比你聰明，他就說過一句這樣有智慧的話：愛情離不開生活！更重要的是，他知道這句話對你的意義是：沒有店，也 沒有婚姻了！

〔每一個人都還在等。〕

楊太太　現在！

〔傳來腳步聲，大家望向門口，但腳步聲過去了，沒有人進來。〕

辛太太　這會是一場騙局，我感覺得出來，也聞得出來，新娘在等婚禮開始，然後新郎在等新娘的表哥。

楊　森　表哥一定會來的。

沈　蒂　（輕輕地）喔，楊森！

楊　森　我口袋裡有兩張車票，旁邊卻坐著一個不懂算術的笨蛋，我料想有一天你會帶著警察到我家裡來，要我交還那兩百塊大洋。

沈　蒂　（對著觀眾）他壞，卻也要我跟著一起壞。我在這兒，我愛他，他在等表哥，可是我周圍卻都是一群脆弱的人：那位老婦人和她那生病的丈夫，早上等在後門口要米的窮人，北京那位正在擔心他的職位的不知名人士，他們都信任我，保護我。

楊　森　（注視著已經空了的玻璃酒壺）這個玻璃酒壺就是我們的時 鐘，我們是窮人家，客人喝了酒，時鐘就停了不走。

〔楊太太做手勢要他安靜，因為又傳來了腳步聲。〕

服務生　（進來）要再來一壺酒嗎，楊太太？

楊太太　不要了，我想我們喝夠了，酒只能讓你暖身而已，不是嗎？

辛太太　而且也不便宜。

楊太太　我每次一喝酒就流汗。

服務生　那麼，要不要把帳結一下？

楊太太　（裝作沒聽到）先生女士們，我要求大家再多忍耐一下子，表哥一定已經在路上了，（對服務生）不要破壞婚禮！

服務生　沒有結帳我不能讓你走。

楊太太　這裡沒有人不認識我！

服務生　沒錯。

楊太太　在這樣的喜日，這真令人掃興，楊森，你說不是嗎？

牧　師　我要走了。（他不高興地離去。）

楊太太　（絕望地）大家不要動，牧師離開一下而已，馬上就回來。

楊　森　算了吧，媽媽。各位先生女士們，既然牧師已經走了，我就不留你們了。

弟媳婦　走吧，爺爺。

爺　爺　（熱切地把杯裡的酒喝光）敬新娘！

姪　女　（對沈蒂）不要和他作對，對他好一點，他很喜歡你。

辛太太　真丟臉！

〔所有客人都離去。〕

沈　蒂　我要不要也走，楊森？

楊　森　不，你等著。（他抓她新娘裝上的飾物拉著她走，把飾物弄得一團亂）這不是你的婚禮吧？我還在等，那老太婆也在等，她要看她的老鷹（指著自己）飛向雲霄！不過現在我看她恐怕得等到聖靈節那天才能走到門口去看她兒子的飛機從她屋頂上飛過。（對著空座位，好像客人還坐在那裡）各位先生女士，你們怎麼不聊天了？大家還喜歡這裡的一切吧？婚禮只不過稍稍拖延一下而已，只因為一位貴客未到，以及新娘還不懂什麼叫做愛的緣故。我，新郎，現在就來唱一首歌給大家助興。（他唱歌）

「聖靈節之歌」

在大家都知道的某一天，
每個人都會大叫「萬歲，
那個可憐女人的兒子要登基為主了！」
那一天就是聖靈節。就在聖靈節那天
他要坐在他的王位上。

就在那天善良會有回報
行惡則付出慘痛代價
功勞和收穫將會微笑和玩耍
互相交換鹽巴和麵包
就在聖靈節那天
互相交換鹽巴和麵包

草原會俯瞰天空
鵝卵石會席捲溪流
人們行善不用眨眼
他們會使得我們的世界像夢幻
就在聖靈節那天
他們會使得我們的世界像夢幻。

就在那天我會成為飛行員
你會成為最好的
你，懶蟲，終於有了工作
你，女人，終於可以休息了，
就在聖靈節那天
你，女人，終於可以休息了。

因為我們幾乎等不到那一天
我知道，這將不會開始
於晚上，七點八點或九點，
而是第一聲的公雞啼叫時。

就在聖靈節那天

第一聲的公雞啼叫時。

楊太太 他不會來了。

〔三個人坐著，其中兩個人一直望著門口。〕

第六場 A

〔老王睡覺的地方，眾神明再度出現在老王的夢中，他趴在一本大書上睡著了，音樂。〕

老　王　我很高興你們來了，大爺們！容我問你們一個深深困擾我的問題，有一位牧師後來改行去水泥廠當工人，我在他住過的一間破茅舍發現了一本書，書中有一段很奇怪的文章，我一定要讀給你們聽，在這兒，（他用左手翻開擺在膝上一本假想的書，這本假想的書底下則是一本真正的書，他拿起假書開始唸，真正的書則還留在膝蓋上）「在松江省有一個地方叫做刺林，那裡種有許多梓樹、絲柏樹、桑椹等等，樹幹圓周幾個指距長的樹就被一些人砍去做狗屋用，樹幹圓周三到四呎長的則被一些有錢人家砍去預備做棺材，另外像樹幹圓周七或八呎長的就被一些人砍去當別墅的横樑，因此這些樹沒有一棵活得過該有的年限，長到一個地步就被鋸子和斧頭給滅 絕了，這叫物盡其用。」

神明丙　這樣看來，最為人們少利用到的該就是最好的。

老　王　不，應該是最快樂的，是最壞也是最快樂的。

神明甲　人們寫這些什麼鬼東西！

神明乙　為什麼這篇寓言會影響你這麼深刻，賣水的人？

老　王　那是因為沈蒂的關係，大爺們！她為了愛而感到憂傷，因為她遵守戒律：愛你的鄰人！也許對這個世界而言，她實在是太好了，大爺們！

神明甲　無稽之談，軟弱可憐的人！你似乎是被卑賤和懷疑的想法給吞噬了。

老　王　是的，大爺，寬恕我！我只是想您也許能夠加以干預。

神明甲　這行不得，你看我們這位朋友（他指著神明乙，他有一邊的眼睛是烏青的），他昨天才干預了人家的一樁糾紛，你看到了下場即是如此。

老　王　可是她老是必須把她表哥叫來，我後來發現她表哥還真是個能幹的人，但也還是無濟於事，那家店眼看著就要完蛋了。

神明丙　（有些憂心）也許我們是不是應該出面幫忙？

神明甲　我堅持她應該自己想辦法。

神明乙　（堅定地）一個好人的處境越壞　，他更能顯露他好的地方，受苦讓人變得高貴！

神明甲　我們所有的希望都寄託在她身上。

神明丙　事情未必會是我們所期待的樣子，時常我們看到一些好的開始、叫人欣賞的企圖心，以及許多高尚的原則等等，但這些並不足以構成一個好人的條件，我們半途上遇到的一些好人，他們的生活都是沒有尊嚴，也沒有人道。（坦白地）我們睡覺的地方真是糟，你看我們身上沾滿稻草就知道我們晚上睡的是什麼樣的地方了。

老　王　只要求一件事情，您可不可以至少……。

眾神明　不，我們是旁觀者，我們堅決相信我們的好女人在這黑暗的世界上會有她自己的辦法的，負擔越重，她的力量就越大！等著瞧，賣水的人，你會看到每件事情都會好起來……。

〔眾神明的身影越來越淡，聲音也越來越輕。現在他們消失了，聲音也聽不到了。〕

第七場

〔沈蒂煙草店的後院，一輛馬車上擺設有一些家庭用具，沈蒂和辛太太正從繩上取下換洗的衣物。〕

辛太太 我真不懂，你應該拼死也要保住你的店才對。

沈　蒂 什麼？我連房子租金都付不出來，那對老夫婦的那兩百塊大洋我必須今天還他們，那筆錢我已經給了別人，所以我只好把煙草賣給梅珠太太。

辛太太 那你就一無所有了，沒有丈夫，沒有煙草，也沒地方住！你要比別人好就會落得如此下場，你今後要靠什麼過活？

沈　蒂 我不知道，也許可以靠捲煙草賺一點吧。

辛太太 蕭大的褲子怎麼會在這裡？他難道是光著身子離開這裡的不成？！

沈　蒂 他有另外一條褲子。

辛太太 我記得你說過他不再回來了，為什麼把這條褲子留下來？

沈　蒂 也許他不要了。

辛太太 要不要我來收走？

沈　蒂 不。

〔師傅先生跑進來。〕

師　傅 什麼都不要說，我知道一切了，你犧牲你的愛情和幸福，只為了不願意對不起信任你的那對老夫婦，真不愧這個地區，這個充滿猜疑和惡毒的地區稱你為「郊區天使」。你的未婚夫達不到你的道德水平，所以你離開他，現在你關閉了你的店，這曾經是多少人的小小避難所！我不能坐視不管，多少個早晨我從我的門口看著你在你的店前面分米給那些可憐的人，那樣的事還會再有嗎？這位四川的好女人消失了嗎？喔，但願你允許我幫你做這些善事！不，什麼都不要說，我不需要任何擔保，也不要什麼聲明說你要求我幫忙！這個，（他拿出一本支票簿，在其中一張上面簽了名，撕下放在馬車上）我給你一張已經簽了名的空白支票，你可以隨意填上任何數目字。現在我要走了，靜靜地，而且是謹慎地，不要求什麼，用腳尖走路，充滿敬意，而且是無私地。（退場）

辛太太 （檢視支票）你得救了！像你這種人總是有好運道，你總是會碰上白痴。現在動手吧，填上一千塊大洋，趁他清醒過來之前我趕快拿去銀行兌領。

沈　蒂 把洗衣服用的籃子放到馬車上，不要那張支票我也付得起洗衣店的帳。

辛太太 什麼？你不要這張支票？這真是罪過！是不是你認為收了這支票就得嫁給他？簡直瘋了！像他這種人會被牽著鼻子走！他們知道這是最大的福氣，還是你仍想黏著你那飛行員？黃街以及這整個地區的人都知道他對你有多壞！

沈　蒂 這都是貧窮所帶來的結果。（對著觀眾）

我看到他睡覺的時候鼓著兩片臉頰，
這可不是好臉頰。
可是早晨時我拿著他的外套，燈光下一照
到處是破洞。
一聽他狡猾的笑聲我就害怕，
可是一看到鞋子上的許多破洞，
我就深深地愛著他。

辛太太 所以發生了這些事情之後你還是護著他，我從未看過像你那樣瘋狂的，（生氣）我看只有把你趕出這個地區，我的呼吸才會順暢些。

沈　蒂　（拿下繩子上的衣物時搖晃著）我覺得有些暈眩。

辛太太　（接過她手上的衣服）你平常伸展四肢或彎腰的時候會覺得暈眩嗎？該不會是肚子裡有小東西在作怪吧？（她笑）真是麻煩！如果真的這樣，那張大支票就報銷了，真不是時候。

〔她拿著籃子走向後面，沈蒂望著她的後面，一動不動，然後看看自己的身體，摸一摸，臉上露出喜悅的表情。〕

沈　蒂　（輕輕地）喔，好高興！一個人正在我子宮裡成長，現在什麼都還看不到，可是確定他已經在那裡，這個世界正秘密地在等他來臨，鎮上的人們這樣說：有人要來了，我們要留意他。

（以表演默劇的方式，她向觀眾介紹她的兒子）飛行員！

歡迎不知名山脈和偏遠地區的新征服者！

他飛越人跡罕至的沙漠去傳遞郵件！

（她牽著小兒子的手走來走去。）來吧，兒子，看看這個世界！這兒，那是一棵樹，鞠躬，問候。（她教他怎麼鞠躬）就是這個樣子，現在你們已經互相認識了。停，賣水的人來了，他是朋友，和他握手，不要怕。請給我兒子一杯水，今天真熱。（她給他杯子）喔，親愛的，警察！我們不要和他打照面，也許我們要在有錢人費彭家的花園裡摘些櫻桃，可是不能讓人看到。來，沒有爹的孩子！你很想要櫻桃的！慢慢來，慢慢來，兒子！（他們小心翼翼地走，四周張望）不，到那邊去，我們可以躲到草叢裡，不，你不能那樣就要跑過去，（他好像拉著她要跑，卻被她拉住）我們不能那麼莽撞，（她突然鬆手）好吧，如果你那樣子的話……（她把他舉高）

可以摘到櫻桃嗎？放到嘴巴裡，那裡最安全，（她向他拿一顆櫻桃塞到自己嘴裡）真是好吃。喔，老天，警察！我們現在非跑不可！（他們逃跑）那裡有條街，很安靜，我們慢慢走以免被人發現，就當沒發生什麼事一般。

（她和小孩走著，她唱歌。）

一顆李子沒緣沒故
打到一個懶鬼，
這個人快快的
就把那顆李子咬住了。

〔賣水的老王出現，手裡牽著一個小孩，他看著沈蒂，覺得很好奇，咳一下。〕

沈　蒂　喔，老王！你好。

老　王　沈蒂，我聽說你現在情況不太好，必須把店賣了才能還債。這是一個無家可歸的小孩，在牲畜欄裡跑來跑去，好像是林吐的小孩，你記得那個木匠嗎？幾個禮拜前他的店倒了，然後就開始喝酒喝個不停，小孩子挨餓，到街上四處遊蕩，能為他們做點什麼嗎？

沈　蒂　（把小孩牽過來）來，小大人！（對著觀眾）

又來了！又有人要求收容，
巧婦真是難為無米之炊！
他的朋友，征服者，你們知道這個人，
是他的辯護者。

（對老王）他可以住師傅先生的小房間，我可能也要去住那裡，我有身了，不要告訴任何人，不要讓楊森知道，免得受他牽制。到城裡去找林吐，告訴他要他來我這兒。

老　王　真是多謝，沈蒂，我知道你會有辦法的。（對小孩）你看，好人總是會絕處逢生，我要趕快去找你父親。（他準備要走）

沈　蒂　喔，老王，我突然想起來，你的手怎麼樣了？我本來想為你作證，可是我表哥……。

老　王　不用擔心我的手，你看，我已經學會不必用右手就可以處理一切事情，我差不多不必用右手了。（他做給她看，不用右 手就可以拿枴杖）看，我做得多好！

沈　蒂　但注意不能讓它僵化了，你現在把馬車拉走，把上面的東西一起變賣，換了錢去看醫生，讓你變得這麼狼狽，真是不好意思。還有，我接受了理髮匠的那些小房間，你覺得怎麼樣？

老　王　無家可歸的人可以住那裡，你自己也可以住，這比我的手要緊，我現在就去找木匠。（退場）

沈　蒂　答應我一定要去看醫生！

〔辛太太回來，跟她招手。〕

辛太太　你瘋了嗎？你把你最後僅有的財產馬車也給人了！他的手跟你有什麼關係？要是讓理髮匠知道，他一定會把你趕出你這最後僅有的避難所，洗衣服的錢你還沒給我！

沈　蒂　你為什麼這麼壞？
你踐踏你的同胞
你們沒有血統關係嗎？
你努力膨脹血管就是為了貪婪。
自然伸展，一隻手自自在在
一方面給予，一方面接受。
貪婪地攫取，要抓緊。哎！

多麼大的誘惑，去給予！
多麼愉快，對人仁慈！
一句好話溜出就像一聲滿足的嘆息。

〔辛太太生氣地走開。〕

沈　蒂　（對小孩）在這兒坐著等你父親來。

〔小孩坐在地上，丈夫和妻子進來，沈蒂開店那天，這對夫妻曾來過，他們這時拖著幾個袋子進來。〕

妻　子　你自己一個人，沈蒂？（沈蒂點頭之後，她把她外甥也叫進來，外甥也拖著一個袋子）你表哥呢？

沈　蒂　他走了。

妻　子　會回來嗎？

沈　蒂　不會，這家店我放棄了。

妻　子　我們知道，所以今天才來，我們手上有幾袋生煙草，是別人欠我們的，我希望能和你的家當一起擺在你的新家，我們現在沒有地方存放，拖在街上走又太招搖，我知道你不會拒絕給這個方便，以前那麼多的麻煩都不會拒絕了。

沈　蒂　我很高興給你們這個方便。

丈　夫　要是有人問起，就說這些煙草是你的。

沈　蒂　誰會問？

妻　子　（瞪著她）譬如說，警察，他們對我們有偏見，老是跟我們作對，這些袋子要擺哪裡？

沈　蒂　我不知道，目前我不想幹任何可能會讓我被抓去關的事情。

妻　子　這是你的作風，可是這是我所僅有的東西了，你不幫忙我們就完了。

〔沈蒂硬不吭聲。〕

丈　夫　想一想，這些煙草可以開創我們的製造事業，可以讓我們維持好一陣子！

沈　蒂　好吧，我替你們保管這些袋子，暫時就擺在後面的房間。

〔她和他們進去後面，小孩看著她進去，然後怯怯地四周張望，走向垃圾桶，翻弄一番，拿食物出來吃，沈蒂和其他人一起出來。〕

妻　子　我猜你一定了解，我們全靠你了。

沈　蒂　我知道。（她看到小孩，呆住了。）

丈　夫　我們後天再來師傅先生的小房間找你。

沈　蒂　你們現在快走，我覺得不舒服。

〔她把他們推出去，三個人退場。〕

沈　蒂　他餓了，他在垃圾桶找食物吃。（他把小該抱起來，接下來述說她對窮人家小孩悲慘命運的恐懼，她讓觀眾看小孩灰白的嘴巴，她保證以後不管怎樣絕不會這樣虐待自己的小孩，她在講話時，樂隊開始演奏「不設防神明和好人之歌」。）

喔，兒子！喔，飛行員！你來到一個什麼樣的世界？
他們讓你在垃圾桶找食物吃，就是你！
只要看看那張灰白的小嘴！
（她抱著小該給觀眾看他的嘴巴。）
你怎樣對待你的後代？
你對你子宮生產的果實沒同情心？

也不同情你自己，不快樂的人們？
即使會成為母老虎我也要好好保護我的小孩！
看了這個之後，從現在起我要和大家隔離！
我將不眠不休救我的兒子，就是他！
我在貧民窟的學校所學到的是打架和欺騙，
現在對你會有用處，吾兒！
我會好好對待你，對別人則像
一隻母老虎，一隻野獸，
如果不得不這樣的話，
但我一定會這樣。

〔她離開，改換表哥的服裝。〕

沈　蒂　（要走時）再一次必須這樣，我希望這是最後一次。

〔她手上拿著蕭大的褲子，辛太太剛好回來，很好奇地望著她背後。弟媳婦和爺爺進場，音樂小聲地繼續著。〕

弟媳婦　店結束了，家具都搬到後院去了，整個結束了。

辛太太　這是輕率、濫情以及自戀的結果。大家往哪兒走呢？下去，下去，下去！一直進到師傅先生的小房間，你也一起。

弟媳婦　她會很吃驚！我們來這裡發牢騷！到處是潮濕的老鼠洞，還有腐朽的地板！理髮匠讓我們住這兒，因為他的肥皂庫存都堆在這兒發霉，他說：「我的地方給你們住，還有什麼話講？」真可恥！我們要講的就是這個！

〔失業者進來。〕

失業者 沈蒂要搬走，真的嗎？

弟媳婦 沒錯，她想溜走，沒有人能找到她。

辛太太 她的店垮了，她覺得丟臉。

失業者 （興奮）她一定要叫她表哥來！建議她叫她表哥來，表哥是唯一有辦法的人。

弟媳婦 這倒是真的，他很精，他得救這個店，然後沈蒂才能夠再幫我們忙。

失業者 我想的不是我們，而是她，但你說對了，她應該叫他來，為她自己，也為我們大家。

〔老王和木匠進來，老王手上牽著兩個小孩。〕

木　匠 真不知道要怎樣感謝你們，（對大家）我們有地方住了。

辛太太 哪裡？

木　匠 師傅先生的小房間！這是小方帶來的改變！（他看著小方）好，你在這兒！「有人在找住的地方，」沈蒂小姐應該這樣說過，然後她立刻為我們找到了住的地方。（對兩個小孩）謝謝你們的弟弟，你們兩個！（木匠和他的兩個小孩對那個小孩鞠躬）我們謝謝你，小朋友！

〔蕭大進來。〕

蕭　大 請問你們在這裡幹什麼？

失業者 蕭大先生！

老　王 你好，蕭大先生，我不知道你回來了，你認識這位木匠，林吐先生，沈蒂小姐答應讓他來住師傅先生的小房間。

蕭　大　師傅先生的小房間目前不方便。

木　匠　這麼說，我們不能住那兒？

蕭　大　那些房間保留著有別的用途。

弟媳婦　你的意思是我們也不能住囉？

蕭　大　恐怕正是如此。

弟媳婦　那我們要上哪兒？

蕭　大　（聳肩）沈蒂小姐去旅行去了，就我對她的了解，她也並不是想對你們撒手不管，未來事情將弄得更為合理一些，沒有服務回報，就不給東西吃，當然，每一個人都會給他工作機會，讓他好好工作，你們現在願意跟我進去師傅先生小房間的人，絕對不會讓你們一無所得。

弟媳婦　你的意思是說，我們得替沈蒂小姐工作？

蕭　大　沒錯，你們的工作是製造煙草，裡面的房間有三包貨物，去拿來！

弟媳婦　別忘了我們也開過店，我們寧可為自己工作，我們自己有煙草。

蕭　大　（對失業者和木匠）既然你們自己沒有煙草，也許願意為沈蒂工作。

〔失業者和木匠沮喪地走進房間，房東太大進來。〕

房東太太　蕭大先生，賣店的事情怎樣了？我帶來了三百塊大洋。

蕭　大　梅珠太太，我決定店不賣了，我要簽租約。

房東太太　什麼？突然間要給飛行員的錢不要了？

蕭　大　不要了。

房東太太　你有租金嗎？

蕭　大　（拿出理髮匠的支票，填好）我這裡有一張一萬塊大洋的支票，師傅先生開的，他對我表妹有意思，梅珠太太，你自己看看。未來半年的房租兩百塊大洋在下午六點鐘之前會到你手上，現在，梅珠太太，容我說聲抱歉，我今天很忙，我要繼續做我的事情。

房東太太　喔，我知道。師傅先生取代了飛行員的位置！一萬塊大洋！可是，蕭大先生，這年頭的年輕女孩真令我訝異，她們善變，而且膚淺。

〔她離去，木匠和失業者拖著三個袋子進來。〕

木　匠　我不懂為什麼要幫你拖這些袋子。

蕭　大　我懂就夠了，你的兒子在這裡胃口很好，他需要吃東西，林吐先生。

弟媳婦　（看到袋子）我大伯來過這裡？

蕭　大　沒錯。

弟媳婦　我想也是，我認得這些袋子，那是我們的煙草！

蕭　大　你最好不要講那麼大聲，這是我的煙草，因為你看到了，這些袋子是從我的房間拿出來的，如果你有任何疑問，我們可以去找警察，打開看看，你想要這個樣子嗎？

弟媳婦　（生氣）不要。

蕭　大　顯然你根本沒有自己的煙草，在這種情況之下，也許該好好抓住沈蒂小姐伸出來的援手吧？現在請高抬貴手指引我前往師傅先生小房間的路。

〔蕭大牽著木匠最小的小孩的手離去，後面跟著木匠，他的另兩個小孩、弟媳婦、爺爺以及失業者。弟媳婦、木匠和失業者等三人拖著袋子。〕

老　王　他是壞人，沈蒂才是好人。

辛太太　我不知道，曬衣繩上有一條褲子不見了，現在居然穿在她表哥身上，其中必有緣故，我很想知道。

〔那對老夫婦進來。〕

老婦人　沈蒂小姐不在這兒嗎？

辛太太　（心不在焉）走了。

老婦人　那就怪了，她有東西要給我們。

老　王　（悲哀地看著他的手）她曾經也想幫我，我的手越來越僵硬了，我敢說她就快回來了，表哥從來不會逗留太久的。

辛太太　他沒有，有嗎？

第七場 A

〔老王睡覺的地方，音樂，在夢中，賣水的人告訴眾神明他的疑慮，眾神明還在繼續他們的長途旅行，看起來像是累了，他們停一下，回頭看向賣水的人。〕

老　王　大爺們，你們突然出現，把我驚醒，這之前我一直在做夢，我夢見我親愛的姊姊沈蒂來到河邊的燈心草叢裡，很沮喪的樣子，許多人在那個地方自殺過，她搖晃地走著，怪怪的，低著頭，好像在拖著什麼軟軟的卻又很重的東西，這讓她陷在泥巴裡。我叫她，她說她必須把規則的包裹帶到對岸，不能弄濕，以免抹去上面的文字，其實，我看不到她有攜帶什麼，但我帶著疑懼想起那次你們找不到住的地方，她收留你們，臨走時，你們對她表示感激，跟她提到偉大美德的事情，喔，真丟臉！我相信你們了解我的憂慮。

神明丙　你想建議什麼？

老　王　少一些規則，大爺們！減輕規則的數量，以壞時機的觀點 看，減掉那些慈善的規則。

神明丙　譬如什麼，老王，譬如什麼呢？

老　王　譬如只要善意，不要愛或是……。

神明丙　但是那相當困難，不幸的人！

老　王　或者像只要公平而不要公正。

神明丙　但這很煞費周章！

老　王　要不然像只要品行端正而不要榮譽。

神明丙　但是，你要知道，這很煞費周章的，很不簡單的，你這懷疑主義者！（眾神累極，繼續上路。）

第八場

〔蕭大的煙草工廠，蕭大已經在師傅先生的小房間裡建立起一個小煙草工廠。欄干後面幾個家庭擠在一起，特別是女人和小孩，這些人包括了弟媳婦、爺爺、木匠以及他的小孩。楊太太進來，楊森跟在後面。〕

楊太太 （對著觀眾）我要告訴你們，眾人敬愛的蕭大先生怎樣運用他的智慧和力量，把我的兒子楊森從一個墮落的無賴變成一個有用的人。這整個地區的人都知道，蕭大先生在牛棚附近開了一家小煙草工廠，但很快就欣欣向榮發展起來。三個月前我覺得有必要和兒子去看他一趟，不久，他答應了我們的請求。

〔蕭大從工廠出來，走向楊太太。〕

蕭　大 我能為您效勞什麼嗎？楊太太？

楊太太 蕭大先生，我想為我兒子說幾句話，今早警察來我們家裡，告訴我們說你以沈蒂小姐的名義要告我們撕毀婚約，還聲明說楊森以不誠實手段侵佔兩百塊大洋。

蕭　大 沒錯，楊太太。

楊太太 蕭大先生，看在神明的份上，能不能再一次以慈悲為懷？那筆錢花掉了，那個飛行職位泡湯了之後，他在兩天之內就把那筆錢花光了，我知道他是個不成材的東西，他已經賣掉我的家具要去北京，把這位老媽媽丟下不管。（她哭了起來）沈蒂小姐有一度還挺看重他的。

蕭　大 你有什麼話說，楊森先生？

楊　森 （陰鬱地）那筆錢花掉了。

蕭　大　楊太太，因為我表妹對你那墮落的兒子還一直執迷不悟，我預備給他另一次機會，我表妹告訴我說她希望誠實的工作會帶來改進，他可以在我的工廠工作，那兩百塊大洋我們將從他的薪水裡頭慢慢扣。

楊　森　那就是工廠和監獄選一個囉？

蕭　大　你自己決定。

楊　森　我猜我大概不能和沈蒂談話吧？

蕭　大　不能。

楊　森　我的地位呢？

楊太太　真是感激不盡，蕭大先生，你真是太好了，神明會保祐你。（對楊森）你不務正業太久了，現在好好做點正經事，直到能夠再度面對你母親為止！

〔楊森跟著蕭大走進工廠，楊太大回到舞台腳燈處。〕

楊太太　前面幾個禮拜楊森會很辛苦，這個工作並不適合他，要出人頭地很難，但第三個禮拜一件小意外會給他帶來轉機。

〔楊森和木匠林吐各自拖著兩袋煙草。〕

木　匠　（停下來，嘆氣，坐在煙草袋上面）我快幹不下去了，我這年紀幹這工作不行了。

楊　森　（也坐下來）你為什麼不乾脆把袋子往他們臉上扔，拉倒算了？

木　匠　那我們靠什麼過活？我甚至都還必須利用小孩去討生活呢，要是沈蒂小姐能看到這個就好了，她是個好人。

楊　森　她是不錯，要是情況沒變那麼糟，我們可能早就舒舒服服在一起了，真想知道她在哪裡，繼續幹活吧，他這個時候通常會出來。

〔他們站起來，楊森看到蕭大走過來。〕

楊　森　一個袋子給我，你這沒用的東西！（楊森從林吐那裡拿一個袋子過來。）

木　匠　真感謝！如果現在她在這裡，看到你怎樣在幫忙一個老頭，你很快就會有好處。喔，真是的！

〔蕭大進來。〕

楊太太　蕭大先生自然會立即看出不會偷懶的好工人是像什麼樣子的，他進來了。

蕭　大　慢著，你！這怎麼回事？你才背一個袋子？

木　匠　我今天有點累，蕭大先生，而楊森他樂意……。

蕭　大　你再回去拿三個袋子，朋友，楊森能夠做的，你也能做，楊森工作認真，你卻要偷懶。

楊太太　（木匠回去拿另外兩袋的時候）當然，蕭大先生沒對楊森說一句話，他的處置是很明智的，下個禮拜六發工資的時候……。

〔一張桌子，蕭大拿著一包錢，站在工頭——以前的失業者——旁邊，工頭發工資，楊森走上前來。〕

失業者　楊森，六塊大洋。

楊　森　對不起，是五塊才對，五塊大洋。（他把工頭手上的名單拿過來）請看，這裡註明六個工作天，錯了，我有一天因為上法庭沒

來上工，（做作虛假地）工錢雖然低賤，可是不是我該得的我就不要！

失業者 好，那就五塊大洋！（對蕭大）真是少見，蕭大先生！

蕭　大 既然只工作五天，這裡怎麼會寫六天？

失業者 我一定弄錯了，蕭大先生，（對楊森，冷冷的）下次再也不會發生了。

蕭　大 （把楊森叫到一旁）前些日子我注意到你對公司很盡職，很賣力，今天我又看到你誠實的一面，工頭為了給工人好處而弄錯工錢，這種事常發生嗎？

楊　森 他在工人之中有許多朋友，大家也很看重他，視他為他們的一份子。

蕭　大 原來如此，好了，好心有好報，你要不要來一點回報什麼的？

楊　森 不要，不過我要指出的事實是我也很聰明，我受過教育，你知道。工頭很受工人的歡迎，但他沒受過教育，他無法了解公司的需要，試用我一個禮拜，蕭大先生，我可以跟你證明我的聰明比我的體力對公司更有價值。

楊太太 這話說得可真對極了，那天晚上我對我兒子說：你是個飛行員，把這個表現出來，即使你現在當了工人，你會起來的！飛吧，我的老鷹！的確，教育和聰明可以從事偉大的事業！沒有這兩者，你如何躋身上層社會？我的兒子在蕭大的工廠裡製造出了奇蹟！

〔楊森兩腿叉開，站在工人後面，工人頭上有一個籃子，裡頭裝有生煙草，他們一路把籃子遞過去。〕

楊　森 嘿，大家應該再賣力一點！籃子要移動得快些！（對一個小孩）

坐在地板上才不會佔太多空間！還有你，對，就是你，你也可以很容易裝作有壓力的樣子！你們這些懶狗，人家花錢請你來幹嘛的？那個籃子快一點！畜生！把爺爺弄到一旁和小孩一起工作！不要偷懶！大家聽我敲打，按節拍動作！

〔他按節拍拍手，籃子移動得更快。〕

楊太太 這些沒有受過教育的人心生怨恨，不斷咒罵，但沒有一樣能阻擋我的兒子執行他的職務。

〔有一個工人開始唱「第八隻象之歌」，其他人附和唱重複部份的曲調。〕

「第八隻象之歌」

金先生有七隻象
然後又有了第八隻。
那七隻都很野，第八隻溫馴，
第八隻象看守大門。
快跑！
金先生有一個森林公園，
天黑前要打掃乾淨，
現在天就快要黑了！

七隻象在打掃森林，
金先生騎第八隻象，
七隻象整天都在勞動，
第八隻象卻靜靜在等待

快挖！
金先生有一個森林公園，
天黑前要打掃乾淨，
現在天就快要黑了！

七隻象每天從早到晚
都要忙著砍樹，
金先生對七隻象很生氣，但是他
給第八隻象兩斗米，
這是什麼意思？

金先生有一個森林公園，
天黑前要打掃乾淨，
現在天就快要黑了！

七隻象他們沒有長牙，
第八隻象有一個長牙，
每次第八隻象咬裂其他七隻象，
金先生就站在那裡很高興。
繼續挖！
金先生有一個森林公園，
天黑前要打掃乾淨，
現在天就快要黑了！

〔蕭大咬著雪茄不時漫步過來，楊森笑著，加入第三節重複曲調部份，最後一節時拍著手把節拍加快。〕

楊太太　我們真的不知道要怎樣感謝蕭大先生才好，他幾乎不費什麼吹灰之力，只用智慧和耐力，就把楊森本性中隱藏的所有好處都挖掘了出來。他不像他那位大家都極為稱讚的表妹那樣只作虛假的承諾，他就是強迫他賣力工作。今天，楊森已經變成了另外一個人，這個你不得不承認！高貴的人就像一個鈴，你要搖它，它才會響，如果你不搖它，它就不響，俗語就是這樣說的。

第九場

〔沈蒂的煙草店，店已經變成一間辦公室，有漂亮的椅子，還舖著精美的地毯。正在下雨，蕭大變得肥胖，正準備要送老夫婦出去，辛太太看著他們，很高興的樣子，她穿著一套新衣服。〕

蕭　大　很抱歉我無法告訴你們她什麼時候回來。

老婦人　我們今天接到一封信以及上回我們借給她的那兩百塊大洋，信封上沒有寄信人的地址，但這一定是沈蒂寄來的，我們想寫信給她，她的地址呢？

蕭　大　很抱歉這個我也不知道。

老　人　我們走吧。

老婦人　她遲早應該會回來的。

（蕭大鞠躬，這對老夫婦離去，顯得憂慮不安的樣子。〕

辛太太　他們太晚收到那筆錢了，現在他們的店沒了，因為他們付不出稅金。

蕭　大　他們為什麼不來找我？

辛太太　人們不喜歡來找你，首先，我猜他們在等沈蒂回來，因為他們當初沒立借據。其次，在那要命的時刻裡，老頭生病發熱，他的老婆必須日夜服侍他。

蕭　大　（他想坐下來，開始覺得不舒服）我又覺得暈眩了。

辛太太　（照料他）已經七個月了！太興奮對你不好，你應該很高興有我在你旁邊，這種情況沒有旁人幫忙照料是不行的。好吧，你最難過的時刻來臨時我會在你旁邊的。（她笑。）

蕭　大　（軟弱地）我能指望這個嗎？

辛太太　我保證沒問題，當然你多少要付出一些代價的。把領子打開，這樣會舒服一點。

蕭　大　（難過地）都是為了這個小孩，辛太太。

辛太太　大家都是為了小孩。

蕭　大　我胖得太快，應該要注意。

辛太太　他們認為那是因為你太有錢了。

蕭　大　不知道小孩子會怎樣？

辛太太　你一天問三次，不會有問題的，只要有錢，他要什麼就有什麼。

蕭　大　是的，（憂心地）永遠不要讓他看到蕭大。

辛太太　永遠不要，只要沈蒂就好。

蕭　大　可是這一帶會謠言四起！賣水的人說的事情！大家都在看著這家店！

辛太太　只要理髮匠不知道就好了，喝一點這水。

〔楊森進來，他穿著一套漂亮西裝，手上還提著一個公事包，他看到辛太太拖著蕭大，吃了一驚。〕

楊　森　我打擾到你們了。

蕭　大　（勉強起來，搖晃地走去門口）明天見，辛太太。

〔辛太太戴上手套，微笑著離去。〕

楊　森　手套！哪裡來的？幹什麼用的？她是不是在詐騙你？（蕭大悶聲不響的）你是不是感情太脆弱了？真是好笑。（他從公事包拿出一張紙）總之，你最近有些不對勁，跟以前不太一樣，情緒不穩，優柔寡斷，你是不是病了？公司的業務有問題，

這是警察那邊寄來的另一封信，他們要關閉我們的工廠，他們說他們最多只能允許法定工人人數的兩倍，這個你恐怕要處理一下，蕭大先生。

〔蕭大心不在焉的看了他一會兒，然後到後面房間拿了一個手提袋出來，他從手提袋拿出一頂禮帽，放到桌上。〕

蕭　大　公司希望業務代表們出去時要穿得體面一點。
楊　森　你為我買了這個？
蕭　大　（冷漠地）戴上去，看看合不合適。

〔楊森顯得驚訝，把禮子戴上，蕭大看看他，幫他把帽子調整好。〕

楊　森　你的僕人！但不要再逃避！你今天要和理髮匠討論新計劃的問題。
蕭　大　理髮匠要求的條件太苛刻。
楊　森　什麼樣的條件太苛刻？請你告訴我。
蕭　大　（顧左右而言他）這些小房間已經夠好了。
楊　森　是的，給下層社會的人在那裡工作是夠好了，但對煙草卻不夠好，太潮濕。開會前我要和梅珠太太談一下她那幾棟房子的問題，如果能弄到那幾棟房子，我們就可以把這些乞丐廢物、不三不四的傢伙統統開除，這些人都不行。我要和梅珠太太喝個茶，把她哄得舒舒服服的，一半價錢就能弄到那些房子了。
蕭　大　（嚴厲地）不，看在公司的名譽和利益的份上，我要你個人的行為含蓄點，規規矩矩地做生意。
楊　森　幹嘛生氣？是不是那些不好聽的流言讓你覺得難堪？

蕭　大　我不在意那些流言。

楊　森　那一定又是下雨的關係了，每次下雨你就心緒不寧，很容易生氣，我想知道為什麼會這樣。

老王的聲音　（從外面傳來）

我正在賣水，賣水，
我站在這裡，在雨中。
為了這一點點水
我可要經歷千辛萬苦。
現在我喊：「買水呀！」
但是沒有人要買水，
口渴得要命，
喝水，付錢……。

楊　森　又是那個他媽賣水的人，他又要來囉嗦了。

老王的聲音　（從外面傳來）四川這一帶都沒好人了嗎？甚至好女人沈蒂一向住的這個廣場也沒有嗎？她哪裡去了呢？幾個月前有一次下雨她還好心跟我買了一杯水呢，她現在去哪裡了？沒有人看到她嗎？沒有人知道她的消息嗎？她有一天傍晚走進這 房子就再也沒出來過。

楊　森　要不要我叫他閉嘴？她去哪裡了干他屁事？對了，我在想這件事你一直不肯說，就是怕我知道。

老　王　（進來）蕭大先生，我再問你一次她什麼時候會回來？她已經離開六個月了。（蕭大默不作聲）這段期間變化這麼多，她沒辦法接受的。（蕭大還是不吭聲）蕭大先生，這個地區謠言四起，都說沈蒂一定是發生什麼事了，我們這些她的朋友都很擔心，發個慈悲給我們她的地址吧！

蕭　大　很抱歉，我現在很忙，王先生，你下禮拜再來吧。

老　王　（興奮地）以前每天早上她的門口都會有米，給有需要的人，最近又開始了！

蕭　大　那又說明了什麼呢？

老　王　那表示沈蒂根本就沒離開這裡，可是……。

蕭　大　可是什麼？（老王不說話）讓我來說吧，這是最後一次了，如果你是沈蒂的朋友，王先生，你就盡量少問她的事情，這就是我的忠告。

老　王　真是好忠告！蕭大先生，沈蒂不見之前曾告訴過我她懷孕了！

楊　森　什麼？

蕭　大　（很快地）胡說！

老　王　（很熱切地對蕭大）蕭大先生，你要相信，沈蒂的朋友們會不斷繼續問關於她的事情的，好人不會那麼容易被忘記的，這種人這年頭不多了。（退場）

〔蕭大一動不動，望著他離去，然後很快走進後面的房間。〕

楊　森　（對著觀眾）沈蒂懷孕了！我要樂瘋了！我一直被蒙在鼓裡！她當時一定告訴了她表哥，然後這混蛋立即把她送走！「在小孩的父親被議論之前，趕快裝好行李離開這裡。」這實在很不應該，很不人道。我有一個兒子了，又有一個姓楊的要來到這個世界上了，會怎麼樣呢？那女孩不見了，我卻留在這裡當奴隸！（他很生氣）我被一頂帽子收買了，（他踐踏禮帽）兇手！賊！綁票者！居然沒有人保護那女孩！（後面房間傳來嗚咽聲，他站著不動）是不是有人在哭 ？誰呢？停了，在哭什麼呢？那隻狡猾狗蕭大是不會哭的！那麼是誰呢？早上門口又出現了米，這是怎麼回事呢？難道那女孩真的在這裡不成？是不是他把她藏了起來？有可能是誰在哭呢？我才要哭呢！如果她真懷孕了，我一定要把她給找出來！

〔蕭大從後面房間出來，走向門口，看著外面的雨。〕

楊　森　你說，她在哪裡？

蕭　大　（舉起一隻手，傾聽著）等一下！現在是九點，今天聽不到什麼了，雨太大了。

楊　森　（揶揄地）你期待聽到什麼？

蕭　大　送郵件的飛機。

楊　森　少無聊了。

蕭　大　聽說你曾經想飛是嗎？現在還想嗎？

楊　森　我對目前的職位沒什麼好挑剔的，你知道，我不喜歡做夜間工作，飛機遞送郵件是夜間工作。我現在對公司很有向心力，畢竟這曾經也是我未婚妻的公司，即使她不在了也是一樣，她真的走了，是嗎？

蕭　大　你幹嘛問？

楊　森　也許我對她的一切仍然耿耿於懷。

蕭　大　我表妹一定很高興聽到這個。

楊　森　不管怎樣，我仍然很擔心她的下落，譬如說，她有可能被關起來鎖住了。

蕭　大　被誰呢？

楊　森　被你！

〔停頓。〕

蕭　大　那你要怎麼辦？

楊　森　我可能要開始對我在公司的職位有意見了。

蕭　大　喔，我懂了，如果說公司，也就是我，肯給你一個適當的位置，你願不願意放棄再探問你以前未婚妻的事情？

楊　森　也許。

蕭　大　你想要什麼樣的新職位？

楊　森　最高的那個職位，譬如說，把你的位置給我，你滾蛋。

蕭　大　可是，如果滾蛋的是你，而不是我呢？

楊　森　我可能會再回來，不是一個人。

蕭　大　怎麼說？

楊　森　我會帶警察來。

蕭　大　帶警察來，可是如果警察發現這裡沒人呢？

楊　森　那麼我相信他們會搜查後面的房間，蕭大先生，我對我心上人的想念是沒有止盡的，為了能夠讓她重新回到我的懷抱，我一定要採取某些行動的。（冷靜地）她現在懷孕了，需要有人在旁邊照應，這件事我要去和賣水的人談一談。（他走開。）

〔蕭大看著他出去，一動不動，然後很快回去後面的房間，他拿出一些沈蒂的東西：內衣、衣服，還有盥洗用具，他對著沈蒂從老夫婦那裡買來的那條披肩看了很久。他把這些東西捆成一包，聽到有聲音，把這包東西放到桌子底下。房東太太和師傅先生進來，他們和蕭大打招呼，然後把雨傘和膠鞋放到一旁。〕

房東太太　秋天快到了，蕭大先生。

師　傅　哀傷的季節！

房東太太　你那位迷人的秘書哪兒去了？好一位厲害的多情種！不過我猜你一定不知道他的這一面，他總是有辦法把調情這種事情和對公司業務的關心結合在一塊，然後帶給你好處。

蕭　大　（鞠躬）兩位請隨便坐。

〔他們坐下，開始抽煙。〕

蕭　大　朋友，一個料想不到的意外迫使我必須趕快進行我們的協商，這個協商關係到我已經在進行的計劃的未來。師傅先生，我的工廠有問題。

師　傅　你的工廠一向就是如此。

蕭　大　現在警方已經公開威脅要關閉我的工廠，要是我不能提出新計劃的協商的話。師傅先生，這關係到我表妹的財產問題，我知道你一直對她很有意思。

師　傅　蕭大先生，我不想和你談你的擴充計劃，我只想談和你表妹一起吃頓晚飯的問題，你卻跟我暗示你有財務上的困難。我把幾個小房間交給你全權處理去收容無家可歸的人，你卻在那裡給我搞工廠，我交給她一張支票，你去兌領了，你的表妹不見了，你接收了一萬塊大洋，還批評說我那些小房間太小，先生，你表妹在哪裡？

蕭　大　師傅先生，別擔心這個，我今天特別告訴你，她就快回來了。

師　傅　快回來？什麼時候？你說「快了」已經說了好幾個禮拜了。

蕭　大　我對你沒有什麼多的要求，我只想問要是我表妹回來了，你可不可能在我的新計劃上面表現出更多的興趣。

師　傅　我已經告訴過你一千次了，我隨時準備和你表妹討論任何事情，和你的話什麼都免談，可是，看起來你好像老是在這件事情上面橫添枝節。

蕭　大　再也不會了。

師　傅　你說，什麼時候？

蕭　大　（不確定）三個月之內。

師　傅　我到時候簽。

蕭　大　可是事情總得先準備一下。

師　傅　你可以先準備，蕭大，要是你能確定你表妹在這段時間之內一

定會回來。

蕭　大　梅珠太太，至於你的部份，你已經準備好向警方確認我可以使用你的廠房？

房東太太　當然，如果你同意把你的秘書讓給我的話。你知道我要的條件已經有幾個禮拜了，（對師傅先生）那年輕人在業務上極有效率，我需要一位這樣的經理。

蕭　大　可是你得知道我目前有許多困難要解決，我不能沒有楊森先生，而且我最近的健康狀況也很不好，我一開始就很願意把他讓給你，只是……。

房東太太　只是什麼？

〔停頓。〕

蕭　大　好吧，他明天到你的辦公室去找你。

師　傅　我很高興你終於下了這個決定，蕭大，要是沈蒂小姐回來了之後，這個年輕人還留在這裡，那是非常不恰當的，我們都知道，他曾經傷害她很深。

蕭　大　（鞠躬）的確，請原諒我在沈蒂和楊森先生的問題上面這樣猶豫不決，真不配當生意人，只是他們曾經一度那麼親近。

房東太太　我們諒解你。

蕭　大　（看向門口）朋友，我們現在就來達成一項協定，在這間小而不體面的店裡，曾經有許多附近的窮人來買沈蒂的煙草，我們，這些她的朋友們，決定開十二家漂亮的新店，未來就 專門賣沈蒂的好煙草。有人告訴我說大家都稱呼為「四川的煙草大王」，實際上我只是為了我表妹的利益在執行這樁生意，這個生意是她的，也是她的子女以及未來的子子孫孫的。

〔從外面傳來群眾的聲音，楊森、老王以及警察進來。〕

警　察　蕭大先生，很抱歉，這地區有許多人要求我來查證一項傳言，這個傳言是從你的公司傳出來的，說你剝奪了你表妹沈蒂小姐的自由。

蕭　大　沒這回事。

警　察　楊森先生作證說，他聽到你辦公室的後面房間傳來哭聲，而他肯定這是女人的哭聲。

房東太太　真是撒謊，我和師傅先生，兩個有頭有臉的市民，我們可以作證沒有人在這裡哭，我們只是靜靜地抽著我們的雪茄。

警　察　很抱歉，上面命令我搜查這個有問題的房間。

〔蕭大把門打開，警察欠身一下，走到房間門口，往裡頭看了一下，然後轉身微笑。〕

警　察　裡頭的確沒人。

楊　森　（一直跟在警察後面）可是我真的聽到哭聲！（他眼睛一亮，看到桌下蕭大剛才放的包裹，他審視包裹）剛剛這裡沒這個！

〔他把包裹打開，露出了沈蒂的衣服及其他物品。〕

老　王　這些都是沈蒂的東西！（他跑向門口，大喊）她的衣物在這 裡找到了！

警　察　（拿起這些衣物）你說你的表妹已經離開了，一包她的東西卻出現在你說的桌子底下，我們哪裡可以找到這女孩，蕭大先

生？

蕭　大　我不知道她的地址。

警　察　這就很遺憾了。

群眾的喊叫聲　沈蒂的東西找到了！煙草大王殺害了她並且滅了屍！

警　察　蕭大先生，我看你必須跟我去局裡一趟。

蕭　大　（向房東太太和師傅先生鞠躬）我要為這樁醜事說聲抱歉，朋友，但四川還是有許多法官，我相信事情很快就會澄清的。（他走出去，警察跟隨其後。）

老　王　發生這樣可怕的兇案！

楊　森　（疑惑不解）可是我明明有聽到哭聲的！

第九場 A

〔老王睡覺的地方，音樂，眾神明最後一次出現在賣水的人夢中。他們變了許多，看起來風塵僕僕，勞累不堪，那是由於長途旅行，又經歷許多不愉快經驗的結果，其中一個帽子不見了，一個腳誤觸狐狸捕捉器斷了，三個人都赤著腳。〕

老　王　你們終於來了！沈蒂的店發生了可怕的事情，大爺們！沈蒂幾個月前又離開了！她的表哥佔據了一切！他今天被捕了，大家都認為他殺害她，然後侵佔她的店，但我不相信，我做了一個夢，夢見她告訴我說她表哥監禁了她。喔，大爺們，你們一定要立刻回來，把她給找出來。

神明甲　這太可怕了，我們的整個尋找過程真悲哀，我們遇見的好人不多，而我們遇見的好人又都是過著非人的生活，我們已經決定把範圍鎖定在沈蒂身上。

神明乙　如果她還好好的話！

老　王　她當然還好，可是她不見了。

神明甲　那就整個完了。

神明乙　控制一下自己！

神明甲　那又怎麼樣？如果找不到她，我們就只好打道回府了。我們所看到的是個什麼樣的世界？到處充滿了悲慘、醜陋以及浪費！連鄉下也不能倖免，許多漂亮的樹木都被砍掉架上了電話線，我們在山的另一頭看到冒出許多濃煙，還聽到隆隆的砲聲，這個世界即使有好人也是無可救藥了。

神明丙　哎，賣水的人，我們的戒律似乎太要命了，我看我們所有的道德守則都要被唾棄了，人們泰然自若地忙碌著，善意只是徒然把他們帶往深淵的邊緣，善行則真正地把他們推入深淵了。（對另兩位神明）你們不得不承認，這個世界不能住了！

神明乙　（激烈地）不，那是人的問題！

神明丙　這個世界太冷酷了！

神明乙　人們太軟弱了！

神明甲　尊嚴，朋友們，尊嚴！兄弟們，我們不必絕望，至少我們發現了一個好人，而是一直維持著好，她只不過是不見了，我們趕快去找她！一個就夠了！我們不是說過只要有一個人能夠忍受這個世界，事情就會變好？單單一個？

〔他們很快地消失掉。〕

第十場

〔法庭，群眾、師傅先生和房東太太、楊森和他母親、老王、木匠、爺爺、年輕妓女、那對老夫婦、辛太太、警察、失業者、弟媳婦。〕

老　人　他太有勢力了。

老　王　他想再開十二家新店。

木　匠　如果說被告的朋友——理髮匠師傅和房東太太梅珠——這些人也都是他的朋友，法官怎能作出公平的判決？

弟媳婦　昨晚有人看見辛太太受蕭大之命帶著一隻肥鵝進去法官的廚房，鵝的油脂還從籃子裡滴出來哩。

老婦人　（對老王）我們可憐的沈蒂是永遠找不到了。

老　王　不，只有神明才能發現事實。

警　察　肅靜！法官來了！

〔三位神明穿著法官的袍子進來，當他們經過舞台上腳燈走向座位時，我們聽得到他們在竊竊私語。〕

神明丙　我們會被發現的，那幾張假證書弄得不像。

神明乙　人們會懷疑原來的法官怎麼會突然鬧消化不良。

神明甲　不會的，那很自然，他吃了半隻鵝。

辛太太　這幾個是新法官！

老　王　而且是很好的法官！

〔神明丙聽到這個，回頭對老王微笑，三位神明坐下來，神明甲用木槌往桌上一敲，警察帶蕭大進來，大家對他發出噓聲，但他仍昂首闊步。〕

警　察　準備好好吃一驚吧，今天的法官不是公正的傅儀正，不過三位新法官看起來也還蠻溫和的。

〔蕭大看到三位神明，昏倒。〕

年輕妓女　怎麼回事？煙草大王昏倒了。

弟媳婦　沒錯，他看到新法官！

老　王　他好像認識他們！我真搞不懂。

神明甲　你就是煙草商人蕭大？

蕭　大　（微弱）是的。

神明甲　你被控為了佔據你表妹的事業而將她殺害，你認罪嗎？

蕭　大　不。

神明甲　（翻閱文件）我們先聽聽本區的警察描述一下被告以及他表妹的名聲。

警　察　（走向前）沈蒂小姐是個好善樂施的女孩，如俗話所說，她自己要生活但也幫助別人生活。蕭大先生則適巧相反，他是個有原則的人，沈蒂小姐的慷慨有時候會迫使他不講情面，他不像他表妹，他很尊重法律，有一次，他表妹好心收容一家人，後來由他揭發這些人竟是一群賊，另外一次是在最後 關鍵時刻裡挽救了他表妹免於作偽證，我所認識的蕭大先生是個守法而值得尊敬的公民。

神明甲　在座各位還有沒有人可以作證被告沒有犯這個罪？

〔師傅先生和房東太太走向前。〕

警　察　（小聲對眾神明）師傅先生，一個非常有影響力的紳士。

師　傅　蕭大先生在四川是一位名氣響亮而且相當受人敬重的生意人，

他同時擔任商業理事會的副總裁，而且很快就要被任命為治安法官。

老　王　（打斷）由你任命！你和他有生意往來！

警　察　（小聲）一個討厭的傢伙。

房東太太　身為社區基金會的總裁，我要求庭上注意以下的一個事實：蕭大先生不只預備要給他的工人提供光線充足的健康工作場所，而且也不斷給殘障之家提供服務。

警　察　（小聲）梅珠太太，傅儀正法官的親密朋友。

神明甲　是的，是的，但是我們現在想聽聽對被告不利的證詞。

〔老王、木匠、老夫婦、失業者、弟媳婦以及年輕妓女等走向前。〕

警　察　這個地區的無賴。

神明甲　好，你們對蕭大平常的行為了解有多少？

喊叫聲　（混雜）他毀了我們！

——他勒索我！

——他教唆我們幹壞勾當！

——魚肉鄉民！

——胡說八道！

——騙人！

——兇手！

神明甲　被告，你有什麼話說？

蕭　大　我只是幫助我表妹生存，大人，我每次來都是因為她的店出現危機，有可能倒閉的時候，我來過三次，從未想過要久待不走，可是這最後一次形勢迫使我留了下來，我除了來處理麻煩，什麼好處都沒得到。我表妹很得人緣，我得罪人，所以大家恨我。

弟媳婦　沒錯，這是實情，大人！（對蕭大）我不想提煙草袋子的事。

蕭　大　為什麼不提？為什麼？

弟媳婦　（對眾神明）沈蒂收留我們，他卻把我們交給警察。

蕭　大　你們偷人家的蛋糕！

弟媳婦　他現在卻扯到麵包師的蛋糕！他只是想把那家店據為己有！

蕭　大　那家店不是公眾的收容所，自私的東西！

弟媳婦　可是我們沒地方去！

蕭　大　你們太多人了！

老　王　他們（指著那對老夫婦）也算自私嗎？

老　人　我們把自己的積蓄投注到沈蒂的店上面，你為什麼害我們的店也倒閉了？

蕭　大　因為我表妹要幫一位飛行員的忙，讓他能飛，我為她弄錢！

老　王　也許她是真的想幫他忙，讓他能飛，可是你的興趣卻在於他在北京有好待遇的差事，你覺得把那家店弄到手還不夠！

蕭　大　租金太高！

辛太太　這是實情。

蕭　大　而且我表妹不懂做生意！

辛太太　這也是實情！她同時也愛上了那個飛行員。

蕭　大　她沒有資格戀愛嗎？

老　王　當然有！可是你為什麼要強迫她去嫁給一個她不愛的人，那邊的那個理髮匠？

蕭　大　她愛的那個人是個無賴。

老　王　（指著楊森）他？

楊　森　（跳起來）明知道他是無賴，你還讓他進你的辦公室工作！

蕭　大　為了改造你！為了改造你呀！

弟媳婦　把他塑造成一個奴工監督！

老　王　當他被改造了之後，你就把他轉賣給她（指著房東太太），她到處宣揚這個！

蕭　大　因為除非她能把他弄去為她服務，否則她不肯把房子讓給我！

房東太太　胡說！請不要扯到我的房子，我已經和你沒什麼瓜葛了，你這兇手！（她感到受辱，惱羞成怒。）

楊　森　（堅持要發言）大人，我要為他說幾句話！

弟媳婦　當然，他是你的雇主。

失業者　他是我所見過的最惡劣的奴工監督，他根本已經徹底墮落了。

楊　森　大人，被告可能真的有把我塑造成你們所說的那個樣子，可是他並沒殺人，他被補的幾分鐘前，我聽到沈蒂在他後面的房間哭！

神明甲　（活潑地）她還活著？確實告訴我們你聽到了什麼？

楊　森　（得意地）哭聲，大人，哭聲！

神明丙　你認得她的聲音嗎？

楊　森　當然，我怎麼會認不得她的聲音呢？

師　傅　是啊，你常把她弄哭啊！

楊　森　我也使她快樂啊，可是那時候他（指著蕭大）打算把她賣給你！

蕭　大　（對楊森）因為你不愛她！

老　王　不愛，就是為了錢！

蕭　大　可是要錢幹什麼，大人？（對楊森）你要她犧牲她所有的朋友，可是理髮匠提供小房間和錢給她去幫助窮人，我只好讓她跟他訂婚，這樣她才能行善。

老　王　可是當你弄到了那張大支票之後，為什麼不讓她去行善？為什麼反而把她的朋友關進你那骯髒齷齪的工廠工作，煙草大王？

蕭　大　為了小孩呀！

木　匠　也為了我的小孩是嗎？你為他們做了什麼？

〔蕭大默不作聲。〕

老　王　你現在不說話了！神明送給沈蒂一個小店，就像是一個行善用的小小噴水池，她每次想做些好事的時候，你總是來破壞她。

蕭　大　（憤怒）我要是不這樣做，那個小噴水池很快就會乾掉，蠢蛋！

辛太太　這是實情，大人！

老　王　如果你不能弄到米，噴水池有什麼用呢？

蕭　大　善行只會帶來毀滅！

老　王　（瘋狂）那麼，惡行會帶來美好的人生，是嗎？你到底對我們的好沈蒂做了什麼，你這壞人？這世上有多少好人，大爺們？她是好人！當那邊那個人打斷我的手的時候，她曾經想為我作證，我現在就為她作證，她是好人，我發誓！（他舉起手做發誓狀。）

神明丙　你的手怎麼了，賣水的人？整隻手都僵硬了。

老　王　（指著蕭大）都是他造成的，他一個人！沈蒂要給我錢去看醫生，然後他來了！你真是她的死對頭！

蕭　大　我是她唯一的朋友！

所有的人　她在哪裡？

蕭　大　她走了！

老　王　去哪裡？

蕭　大　我不說！

所有的人　為什麼她一定要走？

蕭　大　（大叫）因為你們會把她撕成碎片！（突然靜下來，跌在椅子上）我撐不下去了，我要把一切解釋清楚，如果大家都迴避，只留下法官，我就招供。

所有的人　他要招供了！他終於想通了！

神明甲　（用木槌敲桌子）請大家迴避！

〔警察清場。〕

辛太太　（離開時笑著）會讓大家大吃一驚的！

蕭　大　所有的人都離開了嗎？全部？我不能再保持緘默了，我認得你們，大爺們！

神明乙　你到底把我們這位四川的好女人怎樣了？

蕭　大　讓我把這驚人的事實招供出來：我就是她！

神明乙　沈蒂！

沈　蒂　是的，我是蕭大，也是沈蒂，兩個人都是我，
您先前的指令要行善又要活著
像閃電一般把我劈為兩半，
我不知道這是怎麼發生的。
既要對別人好又要對自己好——
我無法同時做到，
既要幫助別人又要幫助自己實在太難了。
哎，您的世界太艱苦了！太多悲慘，太多絕望！
誰幫助迷失的人自己就迷失！
因為沒肉吃要死了誰會不為惡呢？
所有需要的東西——我要從哪裡取來呢？
從我自己！可是這樣我卻完了！
太多的善意把我給拖垮了，
不公正的時候我走路昂首闊步還吃好的肉！
您的世界一定有些不對勁。
為什麼惡意得到好報？懲罰等著好人？
喔，我真想縱容我自己！
而且我還有過一個秘密的經驗，

我的養母用陰溝的水為我洗澡：
這帶給我一雙銳利的眼睛，
可是憐憫之心折磨我，
我看到悲慘時就變成像一隻憤怒的狼。
接著我變了，和善的話語在我嘴裡變成了灰燼。
但是我希望成為「郊區天使」，
給予是一種喜悅，一張快樂的臉，我走在雲端。
責備我：我凡事皆以幫助鄰人為主，
我要愛我所愛，讓兒子免於匱乏，
您的偉大計劃，喔，神明大爺，我太窮也太渺小了。

神明甲　（驚嚇莫名）不要再講了，不快樂的女人！我們該想到的是，我們真高興又找到你了！

沈　蒂　可是我要告訴你們的是，我是壞人，每個人都在談論我的罪行！

神明甲　你是好女人，每一個人都在談論你的善行！

沈　蒂　也是壞人！

神明甲　真是誤會！幾樁不幸的事件！一些沒有心肝的鄰居！熱心過度！

神明乙　可是往後她要怎麼生活？

神明甲　她沒問題，她很堅強，身體又好，她可以撐得起來的。

神明乙　可是你沒聽到她說的嗎？

神明甲　（激烈地）混亂了，非常的混亂！而且不可思議，非常的不可思議！我們要承認我們的戒律太過分嗎？或者應該根本就加以捨棄？（憂鬱地）絕不！這個世界應該改變嗎？如何改變？誰來改變？不！每一樣東西都井然有序！（他突然用木槌敲桌子）那麼現在……（他做了一下手勢，音樂開始，燈光轉為淡紅色）我們可以回去了。

這個小小的世界已經牽絆我們太久，
它的喜悅和哀傷使我們振作和痛苦。
然而，在那上面，星星的上端，
我們會很高興想到你，沈蒂，你這好女人
你見證了我們在凡世的精紳，
你在寒冷的黑暗中提著一盞小燈！
再見！好自為之！

〔他再做另一手勢，天花板敞開，一朵粉紅色的雲彩降下來，三位神明慢慢坐了上去。〕

沈　蒂　喔，不要走，大爺們！不要走！不要丟下我！我如何面對那對善良的老夫婦，他們的店已經沒了？以及賣水的人，他的一隻手已經僵掉了？還有，我要怎樣抗拒我不愛的理髮匠以及我所愛的楊森？而且我現在又身懷六甲，小兒子不久就要出生，他需要養育哩！我不能留在這裡！

〔她轉身帶著搜尋的目光走向門口，其他人準備著要進來。〕

神明甲　你可以做得到的，只要善良，一切都會好轉的！

〔證人們進來，他們看到法官浮在粉紅色雲彩上，都吃了一驚。〕

老　王　趕快表現虔敬！神明在我們之間降臨了！三位大仙來四川要尋找一位好人，他已經找到了一位，但是⋯⋯。

神明甲　不要「但是」！她就在這裡！

所有的人　沈蒂！

神明甲　她並沒有消失，她只是被藏了起來而已，她會和你們在一起，一位好人！

沈　蒂　可是我需要我的表哥！

神明甲　不要太頻繁！

沈　蒂　至少一個禮拜一次！

神明甲　一個月一次，那夠了！

沈　蒂　喔，不要離開，大爺們！我有許多事還沒告訴你們！我非常需要你們！

〔眾神明開始唱歌。〕

「雲彩上消失中的神明三重唱」

我們，哎，不要逗留
超過短暫的一年
如果你注視你的寶貝太久
它就會消失不見。
凡世間真理的黃金光彩
難免為陰影遮蓋而失色
所以我們要離開
回去我們的太虛之中。

沈　蒂　救命！（她的叫聲貫穿著這首歌）

我們熱切的搜尋現在已告結束
我們要回去天堂
四川的好好女人
讚賞，永遠讚賞！

〔沈蒂張開雙手絕望地邁向他們時，他們在上面消失了，微笑著，揮著手。〕

收場白

〔一位演員走到幕前，帶著歉意跟觀眾說話。〕

各位先生女士，請不要生氣！
我們知道本劇仍待改進，
一個黃金傳聞在微風中飄盪，
微風停了，我們的結局卻是難堪的。
我們期待您的認可，
我們希望，哎，我們的作品得到讚賞。
其實我也很失望，帶著惶恐
我們看到落幕了，故事卻未結束。
依您看，那麼，該怎麼處理？
改變人性或者——這個世界？嗯，哪一個？
要相信更大更好的神明或者——不要？
我們凡夫俗子如何既要行善又要富有？
避免災難的正確途徑
你必須自己尋找。仔細想，朋友，
人與人之間要如何和睦相處，
好人——包括女人——要有好報，
一定要，一定要找出適當的方針，
各位先生女士，幫我們找吧！

——劇終——

The Good Woman of Setzuan

DRAMATIS PERSONAE

Wang ▸ *a water seller*

Three Gods

The Man

Shen Te/ Shui Ta

Mrs. Shin

Family of eight

The unemployed

The carpenter

The landlady

The police

The young prostitute

The one prostitute

Yang Sun ▸ *an unemployed pilot*

Mr. Shu Fu ▸ *a barber*

The old man and his wife ▸ *a carpet dealer*

Mrs. Yang ▸ *Yong Sun's mother*

The priest

The waiter

PROLOGUE

[A street. It is evening. Wang, the water seller, introduces himself to the audience.]

WANG: I sell water here in the city of Setzuan. It's a difficult business. When water is scarce, I have to go a long way to find any. And when it is plentiful, I am without income. But in our province there is nothing unusual about poverty. It is generally said that only the gods can still help us. From a cattle buyer who moves around a good deal, I learn to my unutterable joy that some of the highest gods are on their way to our province and may be expected here in Setzuan too. Heaven is said to be very disturbed by all the complaints that have been going up. For three days I have been waiting here at the entrance of the town, especially toward evening, so that I may be the first to greet them. Later, I'd hardly have the opportunity to do so. The gods will be surrounded by important people. They'll be in constant demand. If only I recognize them! After all they needn't come together. Perhaps they'll come separately so as not to be so conspicuous. It can't be those people over there, they are coming from work. (*He looks at passing workers.*) Their shoulders are crushed from all the carrying they do. That fellow there can't possibly be a god either, he has ink on his fingers. At best he's an office worker at a cement factory. Even those gentlemen there (*two gentlemen pass*) don't seem like gods to me. They look like people who're always beating somebody, which gods don't need to do. But look at those three! They're quite a different matter. They're well fed, show no sign of having any occupation, and have dust on their shoes, which means they come from far away. They must be gods. Dispose of me, illustrious ones!

[He throws himself down before them.]

THE FIRST GOD (*pleased*)**:** Have we been expected here?

WANG (*giving them a drink*)**:** For a long time. But I was the only one who knew you were coming.

THE FIRST GOD: Well, we need somewhere to stay the night. Do you know a place?

WANG: A place? Countless places! The whole town is at your service, illustrious ones! What sort of a place do you wish?

[*The Gods look meaningfully at each other.*]

THE FIRST GOD: Take the nearest house, my son! Try the very nearest house first.

WANG: I'm a little afraid of making enemies of other mighty men if I favor one of them in particular. Few people can help us, you see, but almost everyone can hurt us.

THE FIRST GOD: Well then, we order you: take the nearest house!

WANG: That is Mr. Fo over there! Wait just one moment!

[*He runs to a house and knocks at the door. It is opened, but one can see that he is rejected. He returns, hesitantly.*]

WANG: That's annoying. Mr. Fo is not at home just now, and his servants don't dare do anything without orders from him, he's so very strict. He will certainly have a fit when he learns who they turned away, won't he?

THE GODS (*smiling*)**:** He certainly will.

WANG: Well then, another moment! The house next door belongs to the widow Su. She'll be beside herself with joy. (*He runs to the house but apparently is rejected there too.*)

WANG: I'll have to inquire over there. She says she has only one little tiny room and it isn't prepared. I can well understand she's ashamed because some corners of the house aren't so clean. That's what women are like, it's a disgrace. I'll go at once to Mr. Tscheng.

THE SECOND GOD: The little room will be enough. Tell her we're coming.

WANG: Even if it isn't clean? It may be swarming with spiders!

THE SECOND GOD: That doesn't matter. Where there are spiders, there aren't so many flies.

THE THIRD GOD: Never mind. (*Friendly, to Wang*) Go to Mr. Tscheng or some other place, my son. Spiders, after all, rather disgust me.

[*Wang knocks again somewhere and is admitted.*]

VOICE FROM THE HOUSE: Spare us your gods! We have other troubles!

WANG (*back with the Gods*)**:** Mr. Tscheng is quite upset. He has the whole house full of relations and doesn't dare show his face, illustrious ones! Between ourselves I believe there are bad people among them whom he doesn't want you to see. He is too afraid of your judgment, that's the thing.

THE THIRD GOD: Are we so terrible, then?

WANG: Only with bad people, isn't that so? It's well known, isn't it, that the province Kwan has been afflicted with floods for decades?

THE SECOND GOD: Really? Why?

WANG: Well, because there's no religion there!

THE SECOND GOD: Nonsense. It's because they neglected the dam!

THE FIRST GOD: Sst! (*To Wang*) Are you still hoping, my son?

WANG: How can you ask such a thing? I only need to go one house farther along. From there on, there'll be plenty to choose from. Everyone's just itching to put you up. Accidental circumstances, you understand. I go!

[*He begins to leave and then, undecided, remains standing in the street.*]

THE SECOND GOD: What did I say?

THE THIRD GOD: Of course it may really be "accidental circumstances."

THE SECOND GOD: In Schun, in Kwan, and in Setzuan—"accidental circumstances" every time? There aren't any religious people left, that's the naked truth, and you don't want to face it. Our mission has failed, why not admit it?

THE FIRST GOD: We might run across some good people at any moment. We mustn't expect things to be too cozy.

THE THIRD GOD: The resolution said. "The world can remain as it is if enough people are found living lives worthy of human beings." Good people, in other words. The water seller himself is such a person unless I'm very much mistaken. (*He goes up to Wang who is still standing undecided.*)

THE SECOND GOD: He is very much mistaken. When this water man gave us a drink from his measuring cup, I noticed something. Here's the cup. (*He shows it to THE FIRST GOD.*)

THE FIRST GOD: It has two bottoms.

THE SECOND GOD: A swindler!

THE FIRST GOD: All right, count him out. But what does it matter if one person is rotten? We'll find enough yet who'll meet our conditions. We have to find one! For two thousand years, they've been shouting: "The world can't go on as it is, no one on earth can be good and stay good." And now at last we've got to name the people who can keep our commandments.

THE THIRD GOD (*to Wang*)**:** Is it so difficult to find a place?

WANG: Not for you! What are you thinking of? It's all my fault a place wasn't found right away. I'm not going about it properly.

THE THIRD GOD: Surely, that's not so.

[*He goes back.*]

WANG: They're noticing already. (*He accosts a gentlemen.*) Pardon me, worthy sir, for accosting you, but three of the highest gods, whose imminent arrival has been discussed for years by all Setzuan, have now actually appeared. They need a place to sleep. Do not pass by! See for yourself.

One look will suffice. Don't wait, for heaven's sake. It's a chance in a lifetime! Be the first to ask the gods under your roof before they're snapped up by someone else. They will accept.

[*The gentleman has passed by.*]

WANG (*turning to another*)**:** My dear sir, you've heard what's going on. Do you, perhaps, have spare rooms? They don't have to be palatial. It's the good intention that counts.

THE MAN: How should I know what kind of gods you've got there? A fellow that lets people into his house likes to know what he's getting.

[*He goes into a tobacco store Wang runs back to the Three Gods.*]

WANG: I've found a gentleman who'll certainly take you.

[*He sees his cup on the ground, looks toward the Gods in confusion, takes it, and runs back again.*]

THE FIRST GOD: That doesn't sound encouraging.

WANG (*as the Man is coming out of the store again*)**:** Well, what about the rooms for the night?

THE MAN: How do you know I don't live at an inn?

THE FIRST GOD: He's getting nowhere. We can cross Setzuan off the list too.

WANG: They're three of the very greatest gods! Really. Their statues in the temples are very well done. If you go quickly and invite them, they might accept!

THE MAN (*laughing*)**:** You must be trying to find a place for a nice bunch of crooks. (*Exit.*)

WANG (*abusing him*)**:** You squinting scoundrel! Have you no religion? You'll all roast in boiling oil for your indifference! The gods spit on you!

But you'll regret it! You'll have to pay. The whole pack of you, fourth cousins included. You've brought disgrace to all Setzuan. (*pause*) And now only Shen Te the prostitute is left. She can't say no.

[*He calls "Shen Te!" above; Shen Te looks out of the window.*]

WANG: They're here. I can't find any place to put them. Can't you take them in for the night?

SHEN TE: I don't think so, WANG. I'm expecting a gentleman. How is it you can't find any other place?

WANG: I can't tell you now. Setzuan is one big dung heap.

SHEN TE: When he comes I'd have to hide. Then maybe he'd go away again. He's expecting to take me out.

WANG: In the meantime, couldn't we come up?

SHEN TE: Well, you don't have to shout. Can we be open with them?

WANG: No! They musn't find out about your profession. We'd better wait downstairs. You won't go out with the gentleman then?

SHEN TE: I'm not so well off. And if I don't pay my rent by tomorrow morning, I'll be thrown out.

WANG: This is no time for calculations.

SHEN TE: I'm not so sure. Stomachs rumble even on the emperor's birthday. But all right, I'll take them in. (*She can be seen putting out the light.*)

THE FIRST GOD: I think it's hopeless.

[*They step up to WANG.*]

WANG (*starting as he sees them standing behind him*) **:** A place has been found. (*He wipes the sweat off*)

THE GODS: It has? Let's see it then.

WANG: There's no hurry. Take your time. The room still has to be fixed.

THE THIRD GOD: Well then, we'll sit down here and wait.

WANG: I'm afraid there's too much traffic right here. Perhaps we should go over there?

THE SECOND GOD: We like to look at people. That's what we're here for.

WANG: But ... there's a draft.

THE SECOND GOD: Oh, we're pretty tough.

WANG: Perhaps you'd like me to show you Setzuan by night? We might take a little walk.

THE THIRD GOD: We've done quite a bit of walking today already. (*Smiling*) But if you want to get us away from here, you need only say so.

[*They go back.*]

THE THIRD GOD: Is this all right with you?

[*They sit down on a doorstep. Wang sits down on the ground at a little distance.*]

WANG (*taking a deep breath*)**:** You're staying with a single girl. She's the best woman—the best human being— in Setzuan.

THE THIRD GOD: That's nice.

WANG (*to the audience*)**:** When I picked up the cup a little while ago, they looked at me so strangely. Did they notice something? I don't dare look them in the eyes any more.

THE THIRD GOD: You're quite exhausted.

WANG: A little. From running.

THE FIRST GOD: Do people have a hard time of it here?

WANG: Good people do.

THE FIRST GOD (*seriously*)**:** And you?

WANG: I know what you mean. I'm not good. But I don't have an easy time either.

[*In the meantime a gentleman has turned up in front of Shen Te's house. He has whistled several times. Each time Wang starts.*]

THE THIRD GOD (*softly, to Wang*)**:** I think he's gone now.
WANG (*confused*)**:** Yes.

[*He gets up and runs to the square, leaving his carrying pole behind But in the meantime the waiting man has left, and Shen Te has stepped through the door and, softly calling "Wang!" has gone down the street. Wang, now softly calling "Shen Te!," gets no reply.*]

WANG: She's left me in the lurch. She's gone off to get her rent together and now I've no place for the illustrious ones. They're tired and still waiting. I can't go back again and say nothing doing. My own little place, a sewer pipe, is out of the question. Moreover, the gods wouldn't want to stay with a fellow when they've seen through his dishonest dealings. I won't go back. Not for anything in the world. But my carrying pole is lying there. What'll I do? I don't dare to get it. Since I didn't succeed in doing anything for the gods, whom I revere, I'll leave Setzuan and hide from their sight.

[*He rushes off. Shen Te returns. She is looking for Wang on the other side and sees the Gods.*]

SHEN TE: Are you the illustrious ones? My name is Shen Te. It would please me very much if you'd be content with my simple room.
THE THIRD GOD: Where has the water seller gone to?
SHEN TE: I must have missed him.
THE FIRST GOD: He probably thought you weren't coming and didn't dare return to us.

THE THIRD GOD (*picking up the carrying pole*)**:** We'll leave this at your house. He'll be needing it.

[*Led by Shen Te, they go into the house. It grows dark, then light again. It is Dawn. Again led by Shen Te, who lights their way with a lamp, the Gods pass through the door. They are taking leave.*]

THE FIRST GOD: My dear Shen Te, we must thank you for your hospitality. We shall not forget that it was you who took us in. Return the carrying pole to the water seller and tell him that we want to thank him too for showing us a good human being.

SHEN TE: I'm not good. I have to confess something: when Wang asked me to put you up I hesitated.

THE FIRST GOD: Hesitating doesn't matter if only you win out. You must know that you did more than give us a place to sleep. Many—even some of us gods—have been doubting whether good people still exist. To decide that question is the main object of our journey. Now that we've found a good human being, we shall joyously continue on our way. Goodbye!

SHEN TE: Stop, illustrious ones! I'm not at all sure that I'm good. I'd like to be good of course, but how am I to pay my rent? Well, I'll confess it to you: I sell myself in order to live, and even so I can't get along. There are many others who have to do the same. I'm ready to do anything; but who isn't? I'd be happy to honor my father and my mother and speak the truth. It would be nice not to covet my neighbor's house. It would be pleasant to attach myself to one man and be faithful to him. I too should like not to exploit anyone, not to rob the helpless. But how? How? Even when I break only a few of the commandments, I can hardly survive.

THE FIRST GOD: All these, Shen Te, are but the doubts of a good woman.

THE THIRD GOD: Farewell, Shen Te! And give my best regards to the water seller. He was a good friend to us.

THE SECOND GOD: I fear he's none the better for it.

THE THIRD GOD: Best of luck to you!

THE FIRST GOD: Above all, be good, Shen Te! Farewell!

[*They turn to go. They are already waving.*]

SHEN TE (*worried*)**:** But I'm not sure of myself, illustrious ones! How can I be good when everything is so expensive?

THE SECOND GOD: We can't do anything about that. We mustn't meddle with economics!

THE THIRD GOD: Stop! Just one moment! Might she not fare better if she were a little richer?

THE SECOND GOD: We can't give her anything. We couldn't account for it up above.

THE FIRST GOD: Why not?

[*They put their heads together and talk excitedly.*]

THE FIRST GOD (*embarrassed, to Shen Te*)**:** You say you can't pay your rent. We're not paupers and of course we'll pay for the room. Here! (*He gives her money.*) But don't tell anyone we paid. Such an action could be misinterpreted.

THE SECOND GOD: It certainly could.

THE FIRST GOD: But it's allowable. We can pay for the room without misgiving. There's nothing against it in the resolution. Well, goodbye!

[*The Gods quickly go.*]

ACT 1

[*A small tobacco store. The store is not as yet completely furnished and has not opened.*]

SHEN TE (*to the audience*): It's now three days since the gods went away. They said they wanted to pay me for the night's lodging. And when I looked to see what they'd given me, I saw that it was more than a thousand silver dollars. With the money I bought myself a tobacco store. Yesterday I moved in here and I hope now to be able to do a lot of good. There, for instance, is Mrs. Shin, the former owner of the store. Yesterday she came to ask for rice for her children. Today I see her again coming across the square with her pot.

[*Enter Mrs. Shin. The two women bow to each other.*]

SHEN TE: Good morning, Mrs. Shin.

MRS. SHIN: Good morning. Miss Shen Te. How do you like it in your new home?

SHEN TE: Very much. How did your children spend the night?

MRS. SHIN: Oh dear, in a strange house, if you can call that shack a house! The youngest is coughing already.

SHEN TE: That's bad.

MRS. SHIN: You don't know what's bad. You're well off. But you'll learn quite a lot in this dump. What a slum this neighborhood is!

SHEN TE: Didn't you tell me the workers from the cement factory come here at noon?

MRS. SHIN: Yes, but otherwise there isn't a soul that buys here, not even the neighbors.

SHEN TE: You didn't tell me that when you sold me the store.

MRS. SHIN: Don't start blaming me now! First you rob me and my children of

our home and then you call it a dump! And a slum! That's the limit! (*She cries.*)

SHEN TE (*quickly*)**:** I'll get your rice right away.

MRS. SHIN: I also wanted to ask you to lend me some money.

SHEN TE (*pouring rice into Mrs. Shin's pot*)**:** I can't. You know I haven't sold anything.

MRS. SHIN: But I need it. What am I to live off? You took everything away from me and now you cut my throat! I'll leave my children on your doorstep, you cutthroat! (*She tears the pot out of Shen Te's hands.*)

SHEN TE: Don't be angry! You'll spill the rice!

[*Enter an elderly couple and a shabbily dressed young man.*]

THE WIFE: Ah, my dear Shen Te, we've heard you're so well off now. You've become a businesswoman! Imagine, we're without a roof over our heads. Our tobacco store has gone to pieces. We were wondering whether we couldn't spend the night with you. You know my nephew? He's come too. He never leaves us.

THE NEPHEW (*looking around*)**:** A nice store!

MRS. SHIN: What sort of people are they?

SHEN TE: They put me up when I first came in from the country. (*To the audience*) When the little money I had was gone, they threw me out on the street. Perhaps they're afraid now that I'll say no.

They are poor.
They have no shelter
They have no friends
They need somebody
How could one say no?

(*Friendly, to the newcomers*) Welcome! I'll gladly give you shelter. Though I only have one very small room behind the store.

THE HUSBAND: That'll be enough. Don't worry.

THE WIFE (*while she brings tea to Shen Te*)**:** We better settle down back here, so we won't be in your way. I suppose you've chosen a tobacco store in memory of your first home. We'll be able to give you some hints. That's another reason why we came.
MRS. SHIN (*sneering*)**:** I hope customers will come too!
THE WIFE: I guess that's meant for us.
THE HUSBAND: Psst! Here comes a customer.

[*A ragged man comes in.*]

THE RAGGED MAN: Excuse me. I am unemployed.

[*Mrs. Shin laughs.*]

SHEN TE: Can I help you?
THE UNEMPLOYED: I hear you're opening up tomorrow. Things sometimes get damaged when you're unpacking. Don't you have a spare cigarette?
THE WIFE: What nerve, begging for tobacco! He might at least ask for bread!
THE UNEMPLOYED: Bread is expensive. A few puffs at a cigarette and I'll be a new man. I'm all in.
SHEN TE (*giving him cigarettes*)**:** That's important, to be a new man. I'll open the store with you as my first customer. You'll bring me luck.

[*The Unemployed quickly lights a cigarette, inhales; and goes off, coughing.*]

THE WIFE: My dear Shen Te, was that right?
MRS. SHIN: If you open up like this, in three days there'll be no store left.
THE HUSBAND: I bet he still had money in his pocket.
SHEN TE: But he said he hadn't.
THE NEPHEW: How do you know he wasn't lying?

SHEN TE (*angrily*): How do I know he was lying?

THE WIFE (*shaking her head*): She can't say no! You're too good, Shen Te. If you want to keep your store, you must learn to say no, now and then.

THE HUSBAND: Why don't you say it's not yours? Say it belongs to a relative who insists on an exact settlement of accounts. Can't you do that?

MRS. SHIN: That could be done if one wasn't always pretending to be a benefactress.

SHEN TE (*laughing*): Scold, scold, scold! If you're not careful I'll give you notice and pour the rice back.

THE WIFE (*horrified*): The rice is yours, too?

SHEN TE (*to the audience*):

They are bad.
They are nobody's friend.
They begrudge everyone his rice.
They need everything themselves.
Who could scold them?

[*Enter a little man.*]

MRS. SHIN (*seeing him and hurriedly starting to go*): I'll see you tomorrow. (*Exit.*)

THE LITTLE MAN (*calling after her*): Stop, Mrs. Shin! It's you I'm looking for.

THE WIFE: Does she come regularly? Does she have any claim on you?

SHEN TE: She has no claim, but she's hungry: that's more than a claim.

THE LITTLE MAN: She knows why she's running. You're the new owner? Oh, you're filling up the shelves already. But they don't belong to you, see! Unless you pay for them. The rascals who were here before didn't pay for them. (*To the others*) I'm the carpenter, you see.

SHEN TE: But I thought they belonged to the furnishings, which I paid for.

THE CARPENTER: Fraud! It's all a fraud! You're working together with that

Shin woman of course. I demand my hundred silver dollars as sure as my name's Lin To.

SHEN TE: How am I to pay it? I have no more money!

THE CARPENTER: Then I'll have you arrested. You'll pay at once or I'll have you arrested.

THE HUSBAND (*prompting Shen Te*): Cousin!

SHEN TE: Can't it wait till next month?

THE CARPENTER (*shouting*): No!

SHEN TE: Don't be hard, Mr. Lin To. I can't settle all claims at once. (*To the audience*)

A little indulgence and strength is redoubled.
Look, the cart horse stops and sniffs the grass:
Connive at this and the horse will pull better.
A little patience in June and the tree is heavy with peaches in August.
How should we live together without patience?
A short postponement, and the farthest goals are reached.
(*To the Carpenter*) Be patient just for a little while, Mr. Lin To!

THE CARPENTER: And who's patient with me and my family? (*He moves a shelf from the wall as if he wanted to take it with him.*) Pay up, or I take the shelves away!

THE WIFE: My dear Shen Te, why don't you let your cousin settle this affair? (*To the Carpenter*) Write down your claim and Miss Shen Te's cousin will pay.

THE CARPENTER: Cousin! I know these cousins!

THE NEPHEW: Don't laugh like that! I know him personally.

THE HUSBAND: What a man! Sharp as a knife!

THE CARPENTER: All right, he'll get my bill! (*He puts down a shelf, sits on it, and writes out his bill.*)

THE WIFE (*to Shen Te*): If you don't stop him, he'll tear the shirt off your body to get his measly shelves. Never recognize a claim, justified or not, or in two minutes you'll be swamped with claims, justified or not. Throw a piece of meat into a garbage can, and all the mangy dogs of the district will be at

each other's throats in your back yard. What are our law courts for?

SHEN TE: If his work doesn't support him, the law courts won't. He's done some work and doesn't want to go empty-handed. And he's got a family. It's too bad I can't pay him. What will the gods say?

THE HUSBAND: You did your share when you took us in. That's more than enough. (*Enter a limping man and a pregnant woman.*)

THE LIMPING MAN (*to the couple*)**:** Oh, here you are! You're nice relatives! Leaving us standing on the street corner.

THE WIFE (*embarrassed, to Shen Te*)**:** That's my brother Wung and my sister in-law. (*To the two of them*) Stop grumbling. Go and sit quietly in the corner and don't disturb our old friend. Miss Shen Te. You can stay here, she's got nothing against it. (*To Shen Te*) I think we've got to take these two in. My sister-in-law is in her fifth month. Or don't you agree?

SHEN TE: Oh, yes. Welcome!

THE WIFE (*to the two*)**:** Say thank you. The cups are back there. (*To Shen Te*) They just wouldn't have known where to go. A good thing you got the store!

SHEN TE (*laughing, and bringing tea, she says to the audience*)**:** Yes, a good thing I did!

[*Enter the Landlady, Mrs. Mi Tzu, a blank in her hand.*]

THE LANDLADY: Miss Shen Te, I am the landlady, Mrs. Mi Tzu. I hope we'll get on well together. Here is the lease. (*While Shen Te is reading through the lease*) The opening of a little store is a beautiful moment, isn't it, ladies and gentlemen? (*She looks around.*) There're still a few small gaps on the shelves, but it'll be all right. You'll be able to bring me some references, won't you?

SHEN TE: Is that necessary?

THE LANDLADY: I've no idea who you are.

THE HUSBAND: Perhaps we can vouch for Miss Shen Te? We've known her since she came to town and will go through fire for her at any time.

THE LANDLADY: And who are you?

THE HUSBAND: I am the tobacco dealer Ma Fu.

THE LANDLADY: Where's your store?

THE HUSBAND: At the moment I don't have a store. I've just sold it.

THE LANDLADY: I see. (*To Shen Te*) And don't you know anyone else who could give me some information about you?

THE WIFE (*prompting*)**:** Cousin! Cousin!

THE LANDLADY: You've got to have somebody to speak for you if you're coming into my house. This is a respectable house, my dear. Without some assurance I can't even sign the lease with you.

SHEN TE (*slowly, with downcast eyes*)**:** I have a cousin.

THE LANDLADY: Oh, you have a cousin. On the square? Then we can go over there right away. What does he do?

SHEN TE: He isn't living here. He's in another town.

THE WIFE: Didn't you say he was in Shung?

SHEN TE: Mr ... Shui Ta. In Shung.

THE HUSBAND: But I know him! A tall thin fellow?

THE NEPHEW (*to the Carpenter*)**:** You were negotiating with Miss Shen Te's cousin too! About the shelves!

THE CARPENTER (*surly*)**:** I'm just writing out a bill for him. Here it is! (*He hands it over.*) Tomorrow morning I'll be back. (*Exit.*)

THE NEPHEW (*calling after him and glancing at the Landlady*)**:** Don't worry, the cousin will pay!

THE LANDLADY (*examining Shen Te closely*)**:** Well, I'll be very pleased to meet him too. Good morning! (*Exit.*)

THE WIFE (*after a pause*)**:** Now the cat's out of the bag. You can be sure she'll know everything about you tomorrow morning.

THE SISTER-IN-LAW (*softly to the Nephew*)**:** This thing won't last long!

[*Enter a boy leading an old man.*]

THE BOY (*calling over his shoulder*)**:** Here they are.

THE WIFE: Good evening. Grandfather. (*To Shen Te*) The good old man! He must have worried about us. And the boy, hasn't he grown? He eats like ten men. Well, who else did you bring, for heaven's sake?

THE HUSBAND (*looking outside*)**:** Only our niece.

THE SISTER-IN-LAW (*softly to the Nephew while a young girl comes in*)**:** The rats climb onto the sinking ship!

THE WIFE (*to Shen Te*)**:** A young relative from the country. I hope we aren't too many for you. We weren't quite as many when you were living with us, were we? Yes, we got more and more. The less we had, the more there were of us. And the more there were of us, the less we had. But now we'll lock up, or there won't be a moment's peace. (*She locks the door and they all sit down.*) We mustn't disturb you in your business, that's the main thing. Or how can the fire be kept burning? We thought we might arrange matters something like this: during the day the young ones will go off and only grandfather, the sister-in-law, and maybe I myself will stay. The others will look in at the most once or twice during the day, all right? Light the lamp over there and make yourself at home.

THE NEPHEW (*humorously*)**:** If only the cousin doesn't pop up tonight all of a sudden. The strict Mr. Shui Ta!

[*The Sister-in-Law laughs.*]

THE BROTHER (*reaching for a cigarette*)**:** One cigarette won't matter much.

THE HUSBAND: I'm sure it won't.

[*They all help themselves to cigarettes. The Brother hands round a jug of wine.*]

THE NEPHEW: The cousin will pay for it.

THE GRANDFATHER (*seriously to Shen Te*): Good evening!

[*Shen Te is confused by the belated greeting and bows. In one hand she holds the Carpenter's bill, in the other the lease.*]

THE WIFE: Couldn't you sing something to entertain our hostess a little?
THE NEPHEW: Grandfather will start!

[*They sing.*]

THE SONG OF THE SMOKE

THE GRANDFATHER:

There was a time—before old age had bleached my hair—
I hoped I might survive by being clever.
But when does cleverness alone suffice
To fill a poor man's belly? Never, never!
That's why I said: let go!
Watch the grey smoke float
Ever into colder coldness: so
Sails your boat.

THE HUSBAND:

I saw the honest, conscientious man oppressed
So by the crooked path I tried to go.
But that path also leads us only downward
And what to do I don't pretend to know.
And so I say: let go!
Watch the grey smoke float
Ever into colder coldness: so
Sails your boat.

THE NIECE:

The old, I hear, have nothing left to hope for.
Since only time can heal, they're in a fix.
But for the young, I hear, the door is open.
It opens, so they tell me, upon nix.
So I too say: let go!
Watch the grey smoke float
Ever into colder coldness: so
Sails your boat

THE NEPHEW: Where did you get the wine?

THE SISTER-IN-LAW: He pawned the bag of tobacco.

THE HUSBAND: What? That tobacco was the only thing left to us! We didn't even touch it to pay for our lodgings! You swine!

THE BROTHER: Do you call me a swine because my wife is cold? And you had a drink yourself? Give me the jug this minute!

[*They fight. The shelves fall over.*]

SHEN TE (*imploring them*)**:** Oh, spare the store! Don't destroy everything! It's a gift of the gods! Take what there is, but don't destroy it all!

THE WIFE (*skeptically*)**:** The store is smaller than I thought. Perhaps we shouldn't have mentioned it to Auntie and the others. If they come too, it'll be very crowded.

THE SISTER-IN-LAW: Our hostess is cooling off already.

[*There are voices outside and a knocking on the door.*]

SHOUTS FROM OUTSIDE: Open Up! It's us!

THE WIFE: Is that you, Auntie? What are we going to do?

SHEN TE: O hope! My beautiful store! I bought it yesterday and today it's

done for.
The little lifeboat
Is swiftly sent down
Too many people greedily
Reach for it as they drown.

SHOUTS FROM OUTSIDE: Open up!

ACT 1-A

[*Below bridge. The water seller crouches by the river.*]

WANG (*looking around*)**:** Everything's quiet. It's four days now that I've been hiding out. They can't find me, because I'm keeping my eyes open. I fled along their road on purpose. On the second day, they passed the bridge, I heard their steps above me. Now they must be a long way off, and I'm safe.

[*He lies back and falls asleep. Music. The slope becomes transparent and the Gods appear.*]

WANG (*raising his arm to his face as if about to be struck*)**:** Don't say anything! I know it all! I found no one who wants to take you, not in a single house! Now you know! Now you can go on!

THE FIRST GOD: But you did find someone. When you were away, she came. She took us in for the night, she watched over our sleep, and when we left her in the morning she showed us the way with a lamp. You mentioned, her to us as a good woman and she was good.

WANG: So it was Shen Te who took you in?

THE THIRD GOD: Of course.

WANG: And I had so little faith, I ran away! Only because I thought: "She can't come. Because she's not well off, she can't come."

THE GODS:

O weak one!
O well-disposed but weak man!
Where there is need, he thinks, there is no goodness!
Where there is danger, he thinks, there is no courage!
O weakness always to believe the worst!
O hasty judgment! Frivolous despair!

WANG: I'm very ashamed, illustrious ones!

THE FIRST GOD: And now, water seller, do us a favor and go back quickly to the city of Setzuan. Look up the good Shen Te there and give us a report on her. She's well off now. She's supposed to have got some money for a little store so she can follow the inclinations of her heart. Show an interest in her goodness. No one can be good for long when goodness is not in demand. We will continue our journey. We will search and find other people who resemble our good woman from Setzuan; the talk about good people being no longer able to live on our earth will stop. (*They disappear.*)

ACT 2

[*The tobacco store. People sleeping everywhere. The lamp is still burning. A knocking.*]

THE WIFE (*getting up, sleepily*): Shen Te! Someone's knocking! Where is she, anyway?

THE NEPHEW: I guess she's getting breakfast. The cousin will pay for it!

[*The Wife laughs and shuffles to the door. Enter a young man, followed by The Carpenter:*]

THE YOUNG MAN: I'm the cousin.

THE WIFE (*falling from the clouds*): What?!

THE YOUNG MAN: My name is Shui Ta.

THE GUESTS (*shaking each other awake*): Her cousin! But that was a joke, she doesn't have a cousin! Someone's here saying he's her cousin! I don't be lieve it, so early in the morning!

THE NEPHEW: If you're our hostess's cousin, go and get us some breakfast quickly!

SHUI TA (*putting out the light*): The first customers will soon be here. Please get dressed so that I can open my store.

THE HUSBAND: Your store? I thought the store belonged to our friend Shen Te. (*Shui Ta shakes his head.*) What, it isn't her store at all?

THE SISTER-IN-LAW: Then she's cheated us! Where is she, anyway?

SHUI TA: She's been delayed. She wants me to tell you that, now I'm here, she can no longer do anything for you.

THE WIFE (*deeply affected*):And we thought she was good!

THE NEPHEW: Don't believe him! Look for her!

THE HUSBAND: That's what we'll do. (*He organizes the search.*) You and you and you and you, look for her everywhere. Grandfather and us, we'll stay here to hold the fort. In the meantime the boy can get us something to eat. (*To the Boy*) You see the bakery over there on the corner? Sneak over and stuff your shirt full.

THE SISTER-IN-LAW: Take a few of the little light cakes too!

THE HUSBAND: But be careful, don't let the baker catch you! And don't run into the policeman!

[*The Boy nods and goes off. The others finish dressing.*]

SHUI TA: This store has been your refuge. Won't you give it a bad reputation if you steal from the bakery?

THE NEPHEW: Don't pay any attention to him. We'll find her soon enough. She'll give him a piece of her mind.

[*The Nephew, the Brother, the Sister-in-Jaw, and the Niece go out.*]

THE SISTER-IN-LAW (*as she leaves*)**:** Leave us some of the breakfast!

SHUI TA (*calmly*)**:** You won't find her. My cousin regrets of course that she can't abide by the law of hospitality for an unlimited period. But unfortunately there are too many of you. This is a tobacco store and Miss Shen Te has to live off it.

THE HUSBAND: Our Shen Te just couldn't say a thing like that.

SHUI TA: Perhaps you're right. (*To the Carpenter*) The unfortunate thing is that the need in this city is too great for a single person to manage. In that regard, nothing has changed, unfortunately, since someone eleven hundred years ago composed these lines:

The governor, asked what was needed
To help the freezing people of the town, made answer:

"A blanket ten thousand feet long
Which would simply cover all the suburbs."

[*He starts to clean up the store.*]

THE CARPENTER: I see you're trying to put your cousin's affairs in order. There's a little debt, recognized by witnesses, and it needs settling. For the shelves. One hundred silver dollars.

SHUI TA (*taking the bill out of his pocket, not unfriendly*)**:** Don't you think one hundred silver dollars a little much?

THE CARPENTER: No. And I can't make any deductions. I have a wife and children to support.

SHUI TA (*severely*)**:** How many children?

THE CARPENTER: Four.

SHUI TA: Then I offer you twenty silver dollars.

[*The Husband laughs.*]

THE CARPENTER: Are you crazy? The shelves are walnut!

SHUI TA: Then take them away.

THE CARPENTER: What d'you mean?

SHUI TA: They cost too much. I beg you, take the walnut shelves away.

THE WIFE: Well said! (*She laughs too.*)

THE CARPENTER (*uncertainly*)**:** I demand that someone call Miss Shen Te. She seems to be a better person than you.

SHUI TA: Certainly. She's ruined.

THE CARPENTER (*resolutely taking some shelves and carrying them to the door*)**:** You can pile up your tobacco goods on the floor! It suits me!

SHUI TA (*to the Husband*)**:** Help him!

THE HUSBAND (*he also grabs a shelf and, grinning, carries it to the door*)**:** Out with the shelves!

THE CARPENTER: You dog, do you want my family to starve?

SHUI TA: Once more I offer you twenty silver dollars. I don't want to pile up my tobacco goods on the floor.

THE CARPENTER: A hundred!

[*Shui Ta looks indifferently out of the window. The Husband prepares to carry out more shelves.*]

THE CARPENTER: At least don't smash them against the door post, idiot! (*Desperately*) But they were made to measure! They fit this dump and nowhere else! The boards are spoiled, mister!

SHUI TA: Exactly. That's why I'm offering you only twenty silver dollars. Because the boards are spoiled.

[*The Wife squeals with pleasure.*]

THE CARPENTER (*suddenly tired*)**:** I can't keep it up. Take the shelves and pay what you want.

SHUI TA: Twenty silver dollars.

[*He places two large coins on the table. The Carpenter takes them.*]

THE HUSBAND (*carrying back the shelves*)**:** It's enough for a heap of spoiled boards!

THE CARPENTER: Enough, maybe, to get drunk on! (*Exit.*)

THE HUSBAND: We got rid of him!

THE WIFE (*weeping with merriment and drying her tears*)**:** "They're walnut!" "Take them away!" "One hundred silver dollars! I have four children!" "Then I'll pay twenty!" "But they're spoiled." "Exactly! Twenty silver dollars!" —That's how one has to treat those scamps.

SHUI TA: Yes. (*Earnestly*) Go away quickly!

THE HUSBAND: Us?

SHUI TA: Yes, you. You're thieves and parasites. If you go fast without wasting time talking back, you can still save yourselves.

THE HUSBAND: It's best just not to answer him at all. Let's not shout on an empty stomach. I'd like to know where the boy is.

SHUI TA: Yes, where's the boy? I told you before, I don't want him in my store with stolen cakes. (*Suddenly shouting*) Once more: Go!

[*They remain seated.*]

SHUI TA (*calmly again*)**:** As you wish.

[*He goes to the door and bows low. A Policeman appears in the doorway.*]

SHUI TA: I presume I am addressing the officer in the charge of this neighborhood?

THE POLICEMAN: Yes, Mr....

SHUI TA: Shui Ta. (*They smile at each other.*) Nice weather today!

THE POLICEMAN: A little warm, maybe?

SHUI TA: A little warm, maybe.

THE HUSBAND (*softly to the Wife*)**:** If he gabbles until the boy comes back, we're done for!

[*He tries secretly to make some signs at Shui Ta.*]

SHUI TA (*without paying attention to him*)**:** It makes a difference whether one thinks of the weather from a cool store or from the dusty street.

THE POLICEMAN: A big difference.

THE WIFE (*to the Husband*)**:** Don't worry! The boy won't come when he sees the policeman standing in the doorway.

SHUI TA: Why don't you come in? It's really cooler in here. My cousin and I have opened a store. We attach the greatest importance, let me tell you, to being on good terms with the authorities.

THE POLICEMAN (*entering*)**:** You are very kind, Mr. Shui Ta. Yes, it's really cool in here.

THE HUSBAND (*softly*)**:** He's taking him in, specially so the boy won't see him.

SHUI TA: Visitors. Distant acquaintances of my cousin, I hear. They are on a journey. (*They bow.*) We were just about to take leave.

THE HUSBAND (*hoarsely*)**:** Well, we'll be going now.

SHUI TA: I shall tell my cousin that you want to thank her for the rooms but that you had no time to await her return.

[*A noise from the street and shouts of. "Stop thief!"*]

THE POLICEMAN: What's that?

[*The Boy is in the doorway. Various kinds of cakes are falling out of his shirt. The Wife waves him desperately back He turns and starts to go.*]

THE POLICEMAN: Stop, you! (*He takes hold of The Boy.*) Where did you get these cakes?

THE BOY: Over there.

THE POLICEMAN: Oh, theft, is it?

THE WIFE: We didn't know anything about it. The boy did it on his own. (*To the Boy*) You good-for-nothing!

THE POLICEMAN: Mr. Shui Ta, can you clarify the situation?

[*Shui Ta is silent.*]

THE POLICEMAN: Aha. You're all coming to the station with me.

SHUI TA: I'm most distressed that such a thing could have happened in my establishment.

THE WIFE: He was watching when the boy went away!

SHUI TA: I can assure you, officer, I should hardly have asked you in if I'd wanted to conceal a theft.

THE POLICEMAN: That's right. And you will also understand, Mr. Shui Ta, that it's my duty to take those people away. (*Shui Ta bows.*) Go on with you! (*He drives them out.*)

THE GRANDFATHER (*solemnly from the doorway*): Good day!

[*Exeunt all except Shui Ta, who continues to tidy up. Enter The Landlady.*]

THE LANDLADY: So you're her cousin! What does it mean that the police are dragging people away from my house? What right has your Miss Shen Te to turn this store into a house of assignation? That's what happens if one takes in people who only yesterday lived in a two-bit hotel and went begging for bread to the corner bakery! You see, I know everything!

SHUI TA: Yes, I see. You've been told bad things about my cousin. She is accused of having gone hungry! It's a notorious fact that she lived in poverty. She's got the worst possible reputation: that of being poor.

THE LANDLADY: She was a common ...

SHUI TA: Pauper. Let's not mince words.

THE LANDLADY: Oh, please, no sentimental rubbish. I'm speaking about her conduct, not her earnings. There must have been earnings, or this store wouldn't be here. Several elderly gentlemen must have taken care of that. How does one get a store at all? Sir, this is a respectable house! The people who pay rent here don't wish to live under the same roof with such a person. Yes, sir. (*pause*) I'm not a monster but I've got to be careful.

SHUI TA (*coldly*): Mrs. Mi Tzu, I'm busy. Just tell me how much it'll cost us to live in this respectable house.

THE LANDLADY: You're a cool customer, I must say.

SHUI TA (*taking the lease from the counter*)**:** The rent is very high. I assume from the contract that it's payable by the month.

THE LANDLADY (*quickly*)**:** Not for people like your cousin!

SHUI TA: What do you mean?

THE LANDLADY: I mean that people like your cousin must pay the half-yearly rent of two hundred silver dollars in advance.

SHUI TA: Two hundred silver dollars! Sheer usury! How am I to get it? I can't count on a large turnover here. My only hope lies in the sack makers at the cement factory. I've been told they smoke a lot because their work is exhausting. But then, they don't earn much either.

THE LANDLADY: You should have thought of that earlier.

SHUI TA: Mrs. Mi Tzu, have a heart! It's true, my cousin has made the unpardonable mistake of giving shelter to unfortunate persons. But she can improve. I'll see to it that she improves. And, tell me, how could you find a better tenant than one who knows the depths because she comes from them? She'll work her fingers to the bone to pay the rent on time. She'll do everything, sacrifice everything, sell everything, shun nothing, and all the time she'll be as humble as a little mouse and as quiet as a fly. She'll give way to you in anything before she'll go back where she came from. Such a tenant is worth her weight in gold.

THE LANDLADY: Two hundred silver dollars payable in advance or she'll go back on the streets where she came from!

[*Enter The Policeman.*]

THE POLICEMAN: Don't let me disturb you, Mr. Shui Ta!

THE LANDLADY: The police certainly display a great interest in this store.

THE POLICEMAN: Mrs. Mi Tzu, I hope you haven't got the wrong impression. Mr. Shui Ta has done us a service and I'm coming solely to thank him for it in the name of the police.

THE LANDLADY: Well, that's nothing to me. I hope, Mr. Shui Ta, that my proposal will be agreeable to your cousin. I like to be on good terms with my tenants. Good day, gentlemen. (*Exit.*)

SHUI TA: Good day, Mrs. Mi Tzu.

THE POLICEMAN: Are you having difficulties with Mrs. Mi Tzu.

SHUI TA: She's demanding the rent in advance because my cousin doesn't seem to her respectable.

THE POLICEMAN: And you don't have the money? (*Shui Ta is silent.*) But surely a man like you, Mr. Shui Ta, can get credit?

SHUI TA: Perhaps. But how can a woman like Shen Te get credit?

THE POLICEMAN: Aren't you staying?

SHUI TA: No. I can't come back either. I can lend her a helping hand only on my trip through town. I can only ward off the worst. Soon she'll have to rely on herself again. I'm wondering what will happen then? I'm worried.

THE POLICEMAN: Mr. Shui Ta, I'm sorry you're in difficulties with the rent. I must admit that at first we looked at this store with mixed feelings. But your courageous behavior a little while ago showed us what you're made of. The authorities soon find out who they can trust.

SHUI TA (*bitterly*)**:** Officer, in order to save this little store, which my cousin regards as a gift of the gods. I'm ready to go to the very limit permitted by law. But hardness and cunning help only against inferiors. The lines are drawn cleverly. I feel like the man who dealt with the rats, only to find himself with rivers to cross. (*After a little pause*) Do you smoke?

THE POLICEMAN (*putting two cigars into his pocket*)**:** Us fellows at the station would hate to lose you, Mr. Shui Ta. But you've got to understand Mrs. Mi Tzu. Shen Te—let's not beat about the bush—lived by selling herself to men. You can object: what else could she have done? How, for instance, was she to pay her rent? But the fact remains: it isn't respectable. Why not? First: one doesn't sell love—beware of the love that's for sale! Second: it's respectable to go with someone you love but not with someone who's pay ing for it! Third: the proverb says, not for a handful of rice but for love! Well, you'll answer, what good is all this wisdom once the milk is spilt? What can she do? She's got to get hold of her half-year's rent or she'll be back on the streets. And how's she to get hold of the rent? Mr. Shui Ta, I have to tell you, I don't know. (*He's busy thinking.*) Mr. Shui Ta, I've got it! Find her a husband!

[*Enter a little old woman.*]

THE OLD WOMAN: A good cheap cigar for my husband. We'll have been married forty years tomorrow, you see, and we're having a little celebration.

SHUI TA (*politely*)**:** Forty years, and you still want to celebrate!

THE OLD WOMAN: As far as our means allow! We own the carpet store across from here. I hope we'll be good neighbors. We should be. Times are bad.

SHUI TA (*showing her various boxes*)**:** A very old saying, I fear.

THE POLICEMAN: Mr. Shui Ta, we need capital. Well, I propose a marriage.

SHUI TA (*apologetically to the Old Woman*)**:** I've let myself be persuaded to bother this gentleman with my personal worries.

THE POLICEMAN: We can't pay the half-year's rent. Very well. We marry a little money.

SHUI TA: That won't be easy.

THE POLICEMAN: Why not? She's a good match. She's got a small, growing store. (*To the Old Woman*) What do you think about it?

THE OLD WOMAN (*undecidedly*)**:** Yes ...

THE POLICEMAN: An ad in the paper!

THE OLD WOMAN (*reticently*)**:** If the young lady agrees ...

THE POLICEMAN: What should she have against it? I'll make out the ad. One good turn deserves another. Don't think the authorities aren't concerned with the struggling small businessman! You lend us a helping hand and in return we make up a matrimonial ad for you! Ha! ha! ha!

[*He eagerly takes out his notebook, wets the stump of a pencil, and writes away.*]

SHUI TA (*slowly*)**:** It's not a bad idea.

THE POLICEMAN: "What ... decent ... man with small capital ... widower ... not excluded ... wishes ... marriage ... into flourishing tobacco store?" And then we'll add: "am ... pretty ... pleasant appearance." How's that?

SHUI TA: If you don't think that's an exaggeration ...

THE OLD WOMAN (*kindly*)**:** Not at all. I've seen her.

[*The Policeman tears the page out of his notebook and hands it to Shui Ta.*]

SHUI TA: With horror I see how much luck one needs to keep above water. How many ideas! How many friends! (*To the Policeman*) Despite my determination, I was at the end of my tether as far as the store rent was concerned. But then you came and helped me with good advice. Truly, now I see a way out!

ACT 3

[*Evening in the city park. A young man—Yang Sun—in ragged clothes follows with his eyes an airplane which seems to be describing a curve high over the city park. He takes a rope out of his pocket and looks carefully around. As he is going toward a large willow, two prostitutes come along. The one is already old, the other is the niece from the family that has imposed itself on Shen Te.*]

THE YOUNG ONE: Good evening, young gentleman. Coming with me, dearie?
SUN: Perhaps, ladies. If you buy me something to eat.
THE OLD ONE: You're nuts, aren't you? (*To the Young One*) Let's go on. We're only wasting our time with him. He's the unemployed pilot.
THE YOUNG ONE: But no one else will be left in the park, it'll rain in a minute.
THE OLD ONE: You never know.

[*They go on. Sun, looking about, pulls out his rope and throws it round a willow branch. But again he is disturbed The two prostitutes are coming quickly back. They don't see him.*]

THE YOUNG ONE: It's going to pour.

[*Shen Te comes walking along.*]

THE OLD ONE: Look, here comes the monster! She brought disaster to you and your family!
THE YOUNG ONE: It wasn't her. It was her cousin. She took us in and later offered to pay for the cakes. I have nothing against her.

THE OLD ONE: But I have! (*loudly*) Ah, here's our dear rich sister! She's got a store but she still wants to snatch our boy friends away.

SHEN TE: Now don't bite my head off. I'm going to the tearoom by the pond.

THE YOUNG ONE: Is it true you're going to marry a widower with three children?

SHEN TE: Yes, I'm meeting him there.

SUN (*impatiently*)**:** Won't you get going, you whores! Can't a man be at peace even here?

THE OLD ONE: Shut your trap!

[*Exeunt the two prostitutes.*]

SUN (*calling after them*)**:** Vultures! (*To the audience*) Even at this remote spot they don't tire of fishing for victims! Even in the bushes, even when it's raining, they desperately search for customers!

SHEN TE (*angrily*)**:** Why do you swear at them? (*She notices the rope.*) Oh!

SUN: What are you gaping at?

SHEN TE: What's the rope for?

SUN: Go on, sister, go on! I've no money, nothing, not even a penny. And if I had a penny, I wouldn't buy you. First I'd buy a cup of water.

[*It starts raining.*]

SHEN TE: What's the rope for? You mustn't do that!

SUN: What's that to you? Clear off!

SHEN TE: It's raining.

SUN: Don't you try to come under this tree.

SHEN TE (*who stays standing in the rain without moving*)**:** No.

SUN: Sister, leave it, it won't help you. You can't do business with me. You're too ugly for me anyway. Crooked legs.

SHEN TE: That isn't true.

SUN: Don't show them! If it's raining, for heaven's sake come under the tree!

[*She goes slowly under the tree and sits down.*]

SHEN TE: Why did you want to do it?

SUN: Do you want to know? Then I'll tell you: to get rid of you. (*pause*) Do you know what it is to be a flier?

SHEN TE: Yes, I've seen pilots in a tearoom

SUN: No, you haven't. Perhaps you've seen a couple of conceited idiots with leather helmets, fellows with no ear for a motor, no sense for a machine. They only get into a plane because they know how to bribe the manager at the airport. Tell one of them: "Take your plane two thousand feet up, let it fall down through the clouds, and then catch it with one flick of the wrist," and he'll say: "That's not in the contract." If you fly, and you don't land your plane as if you were landing on your own rear end, you are not a flier but a fool. I am a flier. And I'm also the biggest fool for reading all those books on flying in the school at Peking and missing out on one page of one book which says that there's no need for fliers any more. And so I'm a flier with out a plane, a mail pilot without mail. You can't understand what that means.

SHEN TE: I think I can.

SUN: No, I'm telling you, you can't understand it. That means you can't understand it.

SHEN TE (*half laughing, half crying*)**:** When we were children we had a crane with a lame wing. He was friendly and didn't mind our jokes. He strutted along behind us, crying out to us not to run too fast. But in the fall and in the spring when large swarms of cranes were flying over the village, he became very restless. And I could understand why. (*She weeps.*)

SUN: Don't howl.

SHEN TE: No.

SUN: It hurts the complexion.

SHEN TE: I'm stopping.

[*She dries her tears with her sleeve. Leaning against the tree and without turning toward her, he reaches for her face.*]

SUN: You don't even know how to wipe your face properly.

[*He wipes it for her with a handkerchief. Pause.*]

SUN: If you had to stay here so I wouldn't hang myself, you might at least open your mouth.

SHEN TE: I don't know anything.

SUN: Why exactly do you want to cut me down from the tree, sister?

SHEN TE: I'm frightened. I'm sure you only wanted to do it because the evening is so gloomy. (*To the audience*)

In our country
There should be no gloomy evenings.
High bridges over the river
The hour between night and morning
And the long winter: they too are dangerous.
For with all the misery
A little is enough
And men throw away
The unbearable life.

SUN: Talk about yourself.

SHEN TE: What about me? I have a little store.

SUN (*mocking*)**:** Oh, you don't walk the streets, you have a store!

SHEN TE (*determinedly*)**:** I have a store now, but, before, I was on the streets.

SUN: And the store was a gift of the gods, I suppose?

SHEN TE: Yes.

SUN: One nice evening they were standing there and saying: Here's some money?

SHEN TE (*laughing softly*)**:** One morning.

SUN: You're not exactly entertaining.

SHEN TE (*after a pause*)**:** I can play the zither a little, and I can mimic people. (*In a low voice she imitates a man of dignity.*) "Well, think of that, I must have left my money at home!" But then I got the store. And the first thing I did was to give away my zither. Now, I said to myself, I can be as dumb as a fish and it won't make any difference.

I'm rich now, I said,
I walk alone, I sleep alone.
For a whole year, I said,
I'll have nothing to do with a man.

SUN: But now you're marrying one? The one in the tearoom by the pond?

[*Shen Te is silent.*]

SUN: What exactly do you know of love?

SHEN TE: Everything.

SUN: Nothing, sister, (*pause*) Or perhaps you liked it?

SHEN TE: No.

SUN (*without turning toward her, he strokes her face with his hand*)**:** Is that pleasant?

SHEN TE: Yes.

SUN: You're easily satisfied, I must say. What a town!

SHEN TE: Don't you have any friends?

SUN: Lots, but none who want to hear I'm still without a job. They make a face as if someone was complaining that there's still water in the ocean. Do you have a friend maybe?

SHEN TE (*hesitantly*)**:** A cousin.

SUN: Then beware of him.

SHEN TE: He's only been here once. Now he's gone away and he'll never be

back. But why are you talking so despairingly? To speak without hope, they say, is to speak without goodness.

SUN: Just go on talking. A voice, after all, is a voice.

SHEN TE (*eagerly*): Despite the great misery, there are still kind people. Once, when I was little, I fell down with a load of brushwood. An old man picked me up. He gave me a penny too. I've often thought of that. Especially those who don't have much to eat like to give some away. People probably like to show what they can do, and how could they show it better than by being kind? Being wicked is just being clumsy. When someone sings a song or builds a machine or plants some rice, that's really a sort of kindness. And you're kind, too.

SUN: It doesn't seem hard to be kind in your eyes.

SHEN TE: No. Just now I felt a raindrop.

SUN: Where?

SHEN TE: Between the eyes.

SUN: Nearer the right one or nearer the left?

SHEN TE: Nearer the left.

SUN: Good. (*After a while, sleepily*) And you're through with men?

SHEN TE (*smiling*): But my legs aren't crooked.

SUN: Perhaps not.

SHEN TE: Definitely not.

SUN (*tired, leaning against the tree*): I haven't eaten anything for two days or drunk anything for one. So I couldn't love you, sister, even if I wanted to.

SHEN TE: It's lovely in the rain.

[*Wang, the water seller appears. He sings.*]

THE SONG OF THE WATER SELLER IN THE RAIN

I'm selling water, water,
And I stand here in the rain.
For such a little water

I've suffered too much pain.
And I shout: "Buy water!"
But nobody's buying
Parched and dying
And drinking and paying!
Buy water, you dogs!

O how I wish the rain would stop!
Last night in bed I dreamt again
That seven years passed without any rain.
I doled out water by the drop.
O how they shouted: "Water, water!"
Each man who came to my place
I looked him over to see whether
I really liked bis face.
How their tongues hung out!

[*Laughing*]

And now reclining on their backs
The little plants and such
Drink at the udder of the clouds
And never ask: How much?
And I shout: "Buy water!"
But nobody's buying
Parched and dying
And drinking and paying!
Buy water, you dogs!

[*The rain has stopped Shen Te sees Wang and runs toward him.*]

SHEN TE: Oh, Wang, are you back again? I've got your carrying pole at home.

WANG: Thank you very much for keeping it! How are you, Shen Te?

SHEN TE: I'm well. I've met a very clever and brave man. And I'd like to buy a cup of your water.

WANG: Put your head back and open your mouth and you'll have as much water as you want. The willow over there is still dripping.

SHEN TE:

But I want your water, Wang,
The water carried from far
The water that has made you tired
The water that will be hard to sell because it is raining.
And I need it for the gentleman over there.
He is a pilot.
A pilot is bolder than other men.
In the clouds' company!
Braving the great storms
He flies through the skies
And brings to friends in far-off lands
The friendly mail.

[*She pays and runs over to Sun with the cup.*]

SHEN TE (*calling back, laughing, to Wang*): He's fallen asleep. Despair and rain and I have made him tired.

ACT 3-A

[*Wang's sleeping quarters in a sewer pipe. The water seller is asleep. Music. The sewer pipe becomes transparent and the Gods appear to the dreaming WANG.*]

WANG (*radiantly*)**:** I've seen her, illustrious ones! She's still the same!

THE FIRST GOD: We're glad to hear it.

WANG: She loves! She's shown me her friend. She's really well off.

THE FIRST GOD: That's good to hear. Let's hope it will give her strength in her striving toward the good.

WANG: Absolutely! She does as many good deeds as she can.

THE FIRST GOD: What sort of good deeds? Tell us about it, my dear Wang!

WANG: She has a kind word for everyone.

THE FIRST GOD (*eagerly*)**:** Yes, and ... ?

WANG: It seldom happens that anyone leaves her little store without tobacco just because he has no money.

THE FIRST GOD: That doesn't sound bad. Anything else?

WANG: She gave lodging to a family of eight!

THE FIRST GOD (*triumphantly to the Second*)**:** Eight! (*To Wang*) And something else perhaps?

WANG: She bought a cup of water from me, even though it was raining.

THE FIRST GOD: Of course, all these smaller good deeds. That's understood.

WANG: But they run into money. A little store doesn't make so much.

THE FIRST GOD: Yes, surely. But a prudent gardener can produce miracles even on a tiny plot.

WANG: She really does that! Every morning she hands out rice, and believe me, it takes more than half her earnings!

THE FIRST GOD (*a little disappointed*)**:** I'm not saying anything. And for a beginning. I'm not dissatisfied.

WANG: Just think, times aren't exactly good! Once, her store got into difficulties and she had to call a cousin to her aid.

As soon as there was a place that was shielded from the wind
The ruffled birds of the whole wintry sky
Came flying and fought for the place
And the hungry fox bit through the thin wall
And the one-legged wolf tipped the small dish over.

In short, she couldn't manage all the business herself any more. But they all agree that she's a good girl. Everywhere she's called the Angel of the Suburbs already. So much good comes from her store. Whatever the carpenter Lin To may say!

THE FIRST GOD: What does that mean? Does the carpenter Lin To speak badly of her?

WANG: Oh, he only says that the shelves in the store weren't paid for in full.

THE SECOND GOD: What are you saying now? A carpenter wasn't paid? In Shen Te's store? How could she allow that?

WANG: I guess she didn't have the money.

THE SECOND GOD: All the same one pays what one owes. The mere appearance of injustice has to be avoided. First the letter of the commandment must be fulfilled. Then the spirit.

WANG: But it was only her cousin, illustrious one, not she herself!

THE SECOND GOD: Then that cousin must never cross her threshold again!

WANG (*downcast*): I understand, illustrious one! In defense of Shen Te, let me at least say that her cousin is considered a highly respectable businessman. Even the police value him.

THE FIRST GOD: Well, we don't want to damn this cousin without having heard him. I admit I don't understand anything about business. Perhaps one should make inquiries to find out what is customary. But anyway, business—is it so very necessary? They're always doing business nowadays! Did the Seven Good Kings do business? Did the Kung the Just sell fish? What does business have to do with an honest and dignified life?

THE SECOND GOD (*with a bad cold*): In any case such a thing must not happen again. (*He turns to go. The two other Gods turn too.*)

THE THIRD GOD (*the last to turn away, embarrassed*): You must forgive our harsh tone today. We're over-tired and haven't slept enough. Lodgings for the night! The wealthy give us the very best of recommendations to the poor, but the poor don't have enough room.

THE GODS (*moving away, grumbling*): Weak, the best of them! Nothing decisive! Little, little! Everything from the heart, of course, but it doesn't amount to much! At least, she should see that...

[*One no longer hears them.*]

WANG (*calling after them*): Oh, don't be angry, illustrious ones! Don't ask too much all at once!

ACT 4

[The square in front of Shen Te's tobacco store. A barber's shop, a carpet store, and Shen Te's tobacco store. It is morning. In front of Shen Te's store, two of the family of eight, the Grand father and the Sister-in-law, are waiting. Waiting also are the Unemployed and Mrs. Shin.]

THE SISTER-IN-LAW: She didn't come home last night!

MRS. SHIN: Unbelievable behavior! At last this crazy cousin has gone away and madam deigns, now and then at least, to give us a little bit of rice out of all her abundance. But already she's staying out all night, loitering around, God knows where!

[Loud voices are heard from the barber's. Wang stumbles out, followed by the fat barber, Mr. Shu Fu, who is carrying a heavy curling iron.]

MR. SHU FU: I'll teach you to bother my customers with your smelly water! Take your cup and get going!

[Wang reaches for the cup held out by Mr. Shu Fu, who hits him on the hand with the curling iron. Wang cries out with pain.]

MR. SHU FU: There you have it! Let it be a lesson to you! (*He goes puffing back into his store.*)

THE UNEMPLOYED (*picking up the cup and handing it to Wang*)**:** You can report him to the police for hitting you like that.

WANG: My hand's smashed.

THE UNEMPLOYED: Is something broken?

WANG: I can't move it.

THE UNEMPLOYED: Sit down and pour a little water over it!

[*Wang sits down.*]

MRS. SHIN: You get the water cheap, anyway.
THE SISTER-IN-LAW: You can't even get a little linen rag here at eight in the morning. She's got to go out! Adventures! What a scandal!
MRS. SHIN (*gloomily*)**:** She's forgotten us!

[*Shen Te comes down the street carrying a dish of rice.*]

SHEN TE (*to the audience*)**:** I've never seen the town in the early morning before. At this hour I used to lie in bed with a dirty blanket over my head, afraid of waking up. Today I walked among the newspaper boys, among the men who rinse the pavement with water, and among the ox carts that bring fresh vegetables from the country. I've walked a long way from Sun's neighbor hood over here, but I've been getting merrier at every step. I've always been told that if you're in love you walk on clouds, but the best thing is walking on the earth, on the pavement. I tell you, in the morning rows of houses look like rubbish heaps with lights on them. The sky is pink and transparent because there's no dust yet. I tell you, you miss much if you don't love, if you don't see your Setzuan at the hour when it rises from sleep like a sober old craftsman pumping his lungs full of fresh air and reaching for his tools, as the poets say. (*To the waiting people*) Good morning! Here's the rice! (*She distributes the rice, then notices WANG.*) Good morning, WANG. I'm quite light-headed today. On the way home I looked at myself in every shop window, and now I feel like buying a shawl. (*After, hesitating a little*) I'd so much like to be beautiful. (*She quickly goes into the carpet store.*)

MR. SHU FU (*who has stepped out again, to the audience*)**:** I'm quite surprised to note how beautiful Miss Shen Te looks today. She's the owner of the tobacco store across the street and I've never really noticed her before. I've been looking at her for three minutes and I think I'm already in love with her. An incredibly attractive person! (*To Wang*) Clear off, you rascal! (*He goes back into his store. Shen Te, the Old Woman, and her husband the carpet dealer step out of the carpet store. Shen Te is wearing a shawl, the carpet dealer is holding out a mirror.*)

THE OLD WOMAN: It's very pretty and not expensive because it has a little hole at the bottom.

SHEN TE (*looking at the shawl on the Old Woman's arm*)**:** The green one's nice too.

THE OLD WOMAN (*smiling*)**:** But unfortunately not the least bit damaged.

SHEN TE: Yes, that's a shame. I can't spend too much, with my small store. I only take in a little and the expenses are great.

THE OLD WOMAN: It's good deeds that cost you so much. Be careful. In the beginning, every dish of rice counts, doesn't it?

SHEN TE (*trying on the shawl with the little hole in it*)**:** Well, that's how things are. But at the moment I'm light-headed. I wonder if this color suits me?

THE OLD WOMAN: That's a question to put to a man.

SHEN TE (*turning to the Old Man*)**:** Does it suit me?

THE OLD MAN: Why don't you ask ...

SHEN TE (*very politely*)**:** No, I'm asking you.

THE OLD MAN (*also politely*)**:** The shawl suits you. But wear it with the dull side turned out.

[*Shen Te pays.*]

THE OLD WOMAN: If you don't like it, you can always exchange it. (*She pulls her aside.*) Does he have any money?

SHEN TE (*laughing*)**:** Oh no!

THE OLD WOMAN: Then how will you be able to pay the rent?

SHEN TE: The rent? I'd completely forgotten it!

THE OLD WOMAN: I thought as much. And next Monday is the first of the month. I'd like to talk something over with you. You know, my husband and I had a few doubts about the marriage ad after we got to know you. We decided to help you out if it comes to the worst. We've put aside a little money and can lend you two hundred silver dollars. If you wish you can pledge us your stock of tobacco. Of course we don't need a written agreement.

SHEN TE: Do you really want to lend money to a light-headed person like me?

THE OLD WOMAN: Well, to be honest, we might not lend it to your cousin—who's definitely not light-headed. But we don't worry about lending it to you.

THE OLD MAN (*stepping up to them*)**:** Settled?

SHEN TE: I wish the gods could have heard your wife just now, Mr. Ma. They're looking for good people who're happy. And you must be happy helping me, for it was love that got me into trouble.

[*The old couple smile at each other.*]

THE OLD MAN: Here's the money.

[*He hands her an envelope. Shen Te takes it and bows. The old couple bow too. They go back into their store.*]

SHEN TE (*to Wang, holding up her envelope*)**:** This is the rent for half a year! Isn't it just like a miracle? And how do you like my new shawl, Wang?

WANG: Did you buy it for the fellow I saw in the city park?

[*Shen Te nods.*]

MRS. SHIN: Maybe you better take a look at his smashed hand? Never mind telling him your doubtful adventures!

SHEN TE (*taken aback*)**:** What's the matter with your hand?

MRS. SHIN: The barber smashed it with a curling iron in front of our eyes.

SHEN TE (*horrified at her negligence*)**:** And I didn't notice anything! You must go to the doctor this minute or your hand will get stiff and you'll never be able to work properly again. What a terrible misfortune! Quick, get up! Go, quickly!

THE UNEMPLOYED: It's not the doctor he should go to but the judge! He can demand compensation from the barber, he's rich.

WANG: You think there's a chance?

MRS. SHIN: If it's really smashed. But is it?

WANG: I think so. It's swollen up already. Maybe I could get a pension?

MRS. SHIN: Of course you've got to have a witness.

WANG: But you all saw it! You could all testify?

[*He looks round The Unemployed, the Grandfather, and the Sister-in-law sit by the wall of the house and eat Nobody looks up.*]

SHEN TE (*to Mrs. Shin*)**:** But you saw it yourself!

MRS. SHIN: I don't want anything to do with the police.

SHEN TE (*to the Sister-in-law*)**:** What about you?

THE SISTER-IN-LAW: Me? I wasn't looking!

MRS. SHIN: Of course you were! I saw you! But you're afraid because the barber's a big shot.

SHEN TE (*to the Grandfather*)**:** I'm sure you'll testify!

THE SISTER-IN-LAW: His testimony won't be accepted. He's gaga.

SHEN TE (*to the Unemployed*)**:** It might be a matter of a pension for life.

THE UNEMPLOYED: I've been picked up twice for begging. My testimony would only do him harm.

SHEN TE (*not quite believing*)**:** So none of you want to say what happened? His hand was smashed in broad daylight, all of you were watching, and nobody wants to speak! (*Angrily*)

Unhappy men!
Your brother is assaulted and you shut your eyes!
He is hit and cries aloud and you are silent?
The beast prowls, chooses his victim, and you say:
He's spared us because we do not show displeasure.
What sort of a city is this? What sort of people are you?
When injustice is done there should be revolt in the city.
And if there is no revolt, it were better that the city should perish in fire before night falls!
Wang, if no one present will be your witness, I will. I'll say I saw it.

MRS. SHIN: That'll be perjury.

WANG: I don't know if l can accept this. Though maybe I'll have to. (*Looking at his hand, worried*) Do you think it's swollen enough? I think maybe the swelling's gone down now?

THE UNEMPLOYED (*reassuring him*)**:** No, the swelling definitely hasn't gone down.

WANG: Hasn't it? No, I guess it's more swollen, if anything. Maybe my wrist is broken after all! I'd better run to the judge this minute.

[*Carefully holding his hand and looking at it all the time he runs off. Mrs. Shin runs into the barber's shop.*]

THE UNEMPLOYED: She wants to get on the right side of the barber.

THE SISTER-IN-LAW: We can't change the world.

SHEN TE (*discouraged*)**:** I didn't want to scold you. I'm only afraid. No, I did want to scold. Get out of my sight!

[*The Unemployed, the Sister-in-Law, and the Grandfather go off, eating and sulking.*]

SHEN TE (*to the audience*):

They no longer answer.
Where one puts them they stay
And if one sends them away
They quickly go. Nothing moves their hearts.
Only the smell of food can make them look up.

[*An oldish woman comes running in.*]

THE OLDISH WOMAN (*out of breath*): Are you Miss Shen Te? My son. Has told me everything. I am. Sun's mother, Mrs. Yang. Just think, he has a chance now. To get a job as flier. This morning. Just now a letter. Came from Peking. From the manager of the airmail service.

SHEN TE: He can fly again? Oh, Mrs. Yang!

MRS. YANG: But the job. Costs a lot of money. Five hundred silver dollars.

SHEN TE: That's a lot, but money mustn't stand in the way of a thing like that. After all, I've got the store!

MRS. YANG: If you could only do something!

SHEN TE (*embracing her*): If only I could!

MRS. YANG: You would give a talented young man a chance?

SHEN TE: How can they prevent a man from being useful? (*After a pause*) Only I won't get enough, for the store, and these two hundred silver dollars cash are just borrowed. Take them with you at once. I'll pay them back by selling my tobacco stock. (*She gives her the old couple's money.*)

MRS. YANG: Oh, Miss Shen Te, that really is help at the right moment! And they were calling him the Dead Flier of Setzuan, they were all so convinced he'd never do any more flying!

SHEN TE: But we need three hundred silver dollars more for the job. We've got to think, Mrs. Yang. (*Slowly*) I know someone who might be able to help me. Someone who helped me out once before. I didn't really want to call him again, he's so hard and cunning. It would certainly have to be the last time. But a flier's got to fly, that's clear.

[*Distant sound of engines.*]

MRS. YANG: If the man you're talking about could get the money! Look, that's the morning mail plane, going to Peking!

SHEN TE (*decisively*): Wave, Mrs. Yang! I'm sure the pilot can see us! (*She waves with her shawl.*) You wave too!

MRS. YANG (*waving*): You know the pilot who's flying up there?

SHEN TE: No. I know the pilot who shall be up there. He gave up hope but he shall fly, Mrs. Yang. One at least shall raise himself above this misery and above us all! (*To the audience*)

Yang Sun, my lover,
In the clouds' company!
Braving the great storms
Flying through the skies
And bringing to friends in distant lands
The friendly mail.

ACT 4-A

[Before the curtain. Shen Te appears with the suit and mask of Shui Ta in her hands. She sings.]

THE SONG OF THE DEFENSELESSNESS OF
THE GODS AND GOODMEN

In our country
The useful man needs luck.
Only if he finds strong helpers
Can he prove himself useful.
Good men can't help themselves
And the gods are powerless.
Why don't the gods have mines and cannon
Battleships, bombers, and tanks?
Bring down the bad and save the good?
Shouldn't we all give thanks?

[She puts on Shui Ta's suit and takes a few steps in his manner.]

Good men
Cannot long remain good in our country.
Where plates are empty, the diners fight.
Alas, the commandments of the gods
Are no use against want.
Why don't the gods appear in our markets
And, smiling, distribute the plentiful food?
Let every man eat and drink at his pleasure
And be to his brother loving and good?

[*She puts on the mask of Shui Ta and now sings with his voice.*]

To procure a dinner
You must be hard as builders of empire.
Without trampling down twelve others
You cannot help one poor man.
Why then don't the gods speak up in their heaven
And say that they owe the good world to good men?
Why don't they stand by good men with their bombers
Fire their guns and suffer no suffering then?

ACT 5

[*The tobacco store. Shui Ta sits behind the counter reading the paper. He doesn't pay the least attention to Mrs. Shin, who is cleaning up and talking at the same time.*]

MRS. SHIN: A little store like this soon comes to ruin when certain rumors start spreading in the neighborhood. Believe me. It's high time that a decent man like you started looking into this dubious affair between Miss Shen Te and that Yang Sun from Yellow Street. Don't forget Mr. Shu Fu, the barber next door, a man with twelve houses and only one wife, and she's old, only yesterday confessed a certain interest in Miss Shen Te. A very flattering interest, I thought. He even inquired about her means. And that, if I may say so, proves real affection.

[*Since she gets no answer, she finally goes out with the bucket.*]

SUN'S VOICE (*from outside*): Is that Miss Shen Te's store?
MRS. SHIN'S VOICE: Yes, this is it. But today her cousin's here.

[*With the light steps of Shen Te, Shui Ta runs to a mirror. She is just about to start fixing her hair when she notices the mistake in the mirror. She turns away laughing softly. Enter Yang Sun. Behind him comes the inquisitive Mrs. Shin. She goes past him into the back room.*]

SUN: I'm Yang Sun. (*Shui Ta bows.*) Is Shen Te here?
SHUI TA: No, she's not.
SUN: I guess you know what our relationship is? (*He begins to inspect the store.*) A real live store! I always thought she was just talking big. (*He looks with satisfaction into the little boxes and china jars.*) Man, I'm going to fly again!

(*He takes a cigar and Shui Ta gives him a light.*) D'you think we can squeeze another three hundred silver dollars out of the store?

SHUI TA: May I ask if you intend to sell it right away?

SUN: Well, do we have the three hundred in cash? (*Shui Ta shakes his head.*) It was decent of her to come right out with the two hundred. But with three hundred still missing, they won't be much use.

SHUI TA: Perhaps it was rather rash of her to promise you,t he money. It may cost her the store. Haste, they say, is the name of the wind that knocks down the scaffolding.

SUN: I need the money quickly or not at all. And the girl isn't one to keep you waiting either. For one thing or another, you get me?

SHUI TA: I get you.

SUN: Uh-huh.

SHUI TA: May I know what the five hundred silver dollars will be used for?

SUN: Sure. I see I'm to be sounded out. The manager at the Peking airport is a friend of mine from flying school. He can get me the job if I cough up five hundred silver dollars.

SHUI TA: Is not that sum unusually high?

SUN: No. He'll have to fire one of his present pilots. For negligence. And the fellow he has in mind isn't negligent, because he's got a large family. You understand. All this, by the way, in confidence. Shen Te needn't know it.

SHUI TA: Perhaps not. Just one thing—won't that manager sell you out next month?

SUN: Not me. There won't be any negligence in my work. I was unemployed long enough.

SHUI TA (*nodding*)**:** The hungry dog pulls the cart home faster. (*He scrutinizes him.*) The responsibility is very great. Mr. Yang Sun, you ask my cousin to give up her small possessions, to leave all her friends in this town, and to put her entire fate into your hands. I assume you intend to marry Shen Te?

SUN: I'd be prepared to.

SHUI TA: But isn't it a pity, then, to get rid of the store for a few silver dollars? We won't get much for it if we have to sell at once. The two hundred silver dollars you have in your hands would pay the rent for half a year. Wouldn't that tempt you to continue in the tobacco business?

SUN: Would it tempt me? Is Yang Sun, the flier, to be seen standing behind the counter: "Do you wish a strong cigar or a mild one, worthy sir?" That's no business for the Yang Sun's, not in this century!

SHUI TA: Allow me to ask, is flying very profitable?

SUN (*pulling a letter out of his pocket*)**:** Sir, I'd get two hundred and fifty silver dollars a month.! Look at the letter yourself. Here's the stamp and the postmark. Peking.

SHUI TA: Two hundred and fifty silver dollars? That's a lot.

SUN: Do you think I fly for nothing?

SHUI TA: The job seems to be good. Mr. Yang Sun, my cousin has commissioned me to help you to this post which means so much to you. From her own point of view, I cannot see any good reason why she shouldn't follow the inclinations of her heart. She has every right to experience the joys of love. I'm prepared to turn everything here to money. Here comes the landlady, Mrs. Mi Tzu, whom I'll ask to advise me about the sale.

THE LANDLADY (*entering*)**:** Good day, Mr. Shui Ta. I suppose it's about the rent which is due the day after tomorrow?

SHUI TA: Mrs. Mi Tzu, circumstances have arisen which make it look doubtful whether my cousin will keep her store. She's planning to marry, and her future husband (*he introduces Yang Sun*), Mr. Yang Sun, will take her to Peking where they are to start a new life. If I can get enough for my tobacco, I shall sell out.

THE LANDLADY: How much do you need?

SUN: Three hundred down.

SHUI TA (*quickly*)**:** No, five hundred!

THE LANDLADY (*to Sun*)**:** Perhaps I'll be able to help you. How much did your tobacco cost?

SHUI TA: My cousin paid a thousand silver dollars for it and very little has been sold.

THE LANDLADY: A thousand silver dollars! She was gypped of course. I'll tell you something: I'll pay you three hundred silver dollars for the whole store if you move out the day after tomorrow.

SUN: We'll do that. It'll work, old man!

SHUI TA: It's too little.

SUN: It's enough!

SHUI TA: I've got to have at least five hundred.

SUN: What for?

SHUI TA (*to the Landlady*)**:** Allow me to talk something over with my cousin's fiancé. (*Aside to Sun*) All the tobacco here has been pledged to two old people for the two hundred silver dollars which were given to you yesterday.

SUN: Is there a written agreement?

SHUI TA: No.

SUN (*to the Landlady*)**:** We can manage with three hundred.

THE LANDLADY: But I've got to know whether the store is in debt.

SUN: You answer!

SHUI TA: The store is not in debt.

SUN: When can the three hundred be had?

THE LANDLADY: The day after tomorrow, and you can still think it over. You'll get more if you don't sell in such a rush. I'll pay three hundred, but only because I want to do my share in what seems to be a case of young love. (*Exit.*)

SUN (*calling after her*)**:** We'll make the deal! Little boxes, jars and sacks, everything for three hundred and the pain's over. (*To Shui Ta*) Perhaps some other place we can get more by the day after tomorrow?

SHUI TA: Not in such a short time. We won't have one silver dollar apart from the three hundred of Mrs. Mi Tzu. You have the money for the trip and the first few weeks?

SUN: Sure.

SHUI TA: How much is that?

SUN: I'll dig it up, anyway, even if l have to steal it!

SHUI TA: Oh, I see, this money too has to be dug up?

SUN: Don't fall out of your shoes, old man, I'll get to Peking somehow.

SHUI TA: It can't be so cheap for two people.

SUN: Two people? I'm leaving the girl behind. At first, she'll only be a millstone round my neck.

SHUI TA: I see.

SUN: Why d'you look at me as if I was a leaking oil tank? You've got to manage the best you can.

SHUI TA: And how is my cousin to live?

SUN: Can't you do something for her?

SHUI TA: I'll try. (*pause*) I wish, Mr. Yang Sun, you'd hand over to me the two hundred silver dollars and would leave them here till you can show me two tickets to Peking.

SUN: My dear man, I wish you'd mind your own business.

SHUI TA: Miss Shen Te ...

SUN: Just leave the girl to me.

SHUI TA: ... might not want to sell her store when she learns that. ..

SUN: She'll want to. Even then.

SHUI TA: And you're not afraid of my interference?

SUN: My dear sir!

SHUI TA: You seem to forget she's a human being and has got some sense.

SUN (*amused*)**:** What certain people think about their female relatives and the effect of reasonable persuasion has always been a source of wonder to me. Have you ever heard of the power of love? The tickling of the flesh? You want to talk reason to her? She doesn't know what reason is! On the other hand, the poor creature's been abused all her life. I've only to put my hand on her shoulder and say "you're coming with me" and she hears bells and wouldn't know her own mother.

SHUI TA (*with difficulty*)**:** Mr. Yang Sun!

SUN: Mr. What's-your-name!

SHUI TA: My cousin is devoted to you because ...

SUN: Shall we say because I've got my hand on her bosom? Put that in your pipe and smoke it! (*He takes another cigar, then puts a few in his pocket, and finally takes the whole box under his arm.*) Don't you go to her with empty hands. We'll stick to the marriage. And she'll bring the three hundred or you'll bring them. Either she or you! (*Exit.*)

MRS. SHIN (*putting her head out of the back room*)**:** Not exactly pleasant. And all of Yellow Street knows he's got the girl completely under his thumb.

SHUI TA (*crying out*)**:** The store's gone! He isn't in love! I'm lost! (*He begins to run round like an imprisoned animal, repeating, "The store's gone!" until he stops suddenly and begins to talk to Mrs. Shin.*) Shin, you grew up in the gutter and so did I. Are we frivolous? No. Do we lack the necessary brutality? No. I'm ready to take you by the throat and shake you till you spit out the last crumb of cheese you've stolen from me. You know that. The times are terrible, this town is hell, but gradually we manage to crawl up the smooth walls. Then bad luck overtakes one or another of us: he is in love. That's enough, he's lost. One weakness and you're finished. How are you to free yourself of all weaknesses, and especially of the deadliest of weaknesses, love? Love is absolutely impossible! It's much too expensive! But then, tell me yourself, can one live and be always on the watch? What sort of a world is this?

Caresses turn to strangulation.
The sigh of love turns to a cry of fear.
Why are the vultures circling over there?
A girl is going to meet her lover.

MRS. SHIN: I think I better go and get the barber right away. You've got to talk with the barber. He's a man of honor. The barber, he's the right one for your cousin.

[*Receiving no answer she runs off. Shui Ta runs around again until Mr. Shu Fu enters, followed by Mrs. Shin, who, however, on a sign from Mr. Shu Fu, is forced to withdraw.*]

SHUI TA (*hurrying toward him*): My dear sir, I know from hearsay that you have hinted at a certain interest in my cousin. Let me set aside all the laws of propriety and reserve: Miss Shen Te is at the moment in great danger.

MR. SHU FU: Oh!

SHUI TA: Only a few hours ago the possessor of her own store, my cousin is now little more than a beggar. Mr. Shu Fu, this store is ruined.

MR. SHU FU: Mr. Shui Ta, the charm of Miss Shen Te lies not in the goodness of her store but in the goodness of her heart. The name which this neighbor hood has given to the young lady tells all. They call her the Angel of the Suburbs!

SHUI TA: My dear sir, this goodness has cost my cousin two hundred silver dollars on a single day. We have to put a stop to that.

MR. SHU FU: Allow me to express a different opinion: we've got to open the gates wide to this goodness. It's in the nature of the young lady to do good. Every morning I affectionately watch her feeding four people. What does that signify? Why can't she feed four hundred? I hear, for instance, that she's racking her brains about how to shelter some homeless people. My cabins behind the cattle run are empty. They're at her disposal. And so on and so forth ... Mr. Shui Ta, might I hope that Miss Shen Te would lend an ear to certain ideas which have come to me in the last few days? Ideas like these?

SHUI TA: Mr. Shu Fu, she will listen to such high thoughts with admiration.

[*Enter Wang with the Policeman. Mr. Shu Fu turns around and studies the shelves.*]

WANG: Is Miss Shen Te here?

SHUI TA: No.

WANG: I am Wang, the water seller. I guess you're Mr. Shui Ta?

SHUI TA: Quite right. Good day, Wang.

WANG: I'm a friend of Shen Te's.

SHUI TA: You're one of her oldest friends, I know.

WANG (*to the Policeman*)**:** You see? (*To Shui Ta*) I'm coming because of my hand.

THE POLICEMAN: It's smashed all right. There's no doubt about it.

SHUI TA (*quickly*)**:** I see you need a sling. (*He gets a shawl from the back room and throws it to Wang.*)

WANG: But that's her new shawl.

SHUI TA: She no longer needs it.

WANG: But she bought it to please a certain person.

SHUI TA: As things have turned out, that is no longer necessary.

WANG (*making himself a sling out of the shawl*)**:** She's my only witness.

THE POLICEMAN: Your cousin's supposed to've seen how the barber Shu Fu hit the water seller with the curling iron. D'you know anything about it?

SHUI TA: I only know that my cousin wasn't present when the incident occurred.

WANG: That's a misunderstanding! Just wait till Shen Te's here and everything will be cleared up. Shen Te'll bear witness to everything. Where is she?

SHUI TA (*seriously*)**:** Mr. Wang, you call yourself my cousin's friend. My cousin has a lot of worries right now. She's been terribly exploited from all sides. In the future, she won't be able to afford the smallest weakness. I'm con vinced you won't ask her to lose all she has by making her say anything but the truth in this matter.

WANG (*confused*)**:** But she advised me to go to the judge.

SHUI TA: Was the judge supposed to heal your hand? (*Mr. Shu Fu turns round.*) Mr. Wang, it's one of my principles never to meddle in the quarrels of my friends. (*Shui Ta bows to Mr. Shu Fu who returns the bow.*)

WANG (*taking off the sling and putting it back, sadly*)**:** I understand.

THE POLICEMAN: And now I guess I can go again. You went to a decent man-the wrong fellow for your swindling. You better be a bit more careful next time, with your accusations. If Mr. Shu Fu didn't put mercy before justice, you could be jailed for libel. Off with you now. (*Exeunt.*)

SHUI TA: I beg you to excuse this occurrence.

MR. SHU FU: It's excused. (*Urgently*) And this affair with a "certain person" (*he points to the shawl*) is really over? Completely finished?

SHUI TA: Completely. She's seen through him. Of course, it'll take time till she's got over everything.

MR. SHU FU: We shall be careful. Delicate.

SHUI TA: There are some fresh wounds.

MR. SHU FU: She'll go to the country.

SHUI TA: For some weeks. However, before that she'll be glad to talk everything over with someone she can trust.

MR. SHU FU: At a small dinner in a small but good restaurant.

SHUI TA: In a discreet way. I'll hurry to inform my cousin. She'll be reasonable. She's very worried about the store, which she regards as a gift of the gods. Be patient for a few minutes. (*Exit into the back room.*)

MRS. SIDN (*putting her head in*): May I congratulate you?

MR. SHU FU: Mrs. Shin, you may let Miss Shen Te's protégés know today that I am giving them shelter in the cabins behind the cattle run.

[*She nods, grinning.*]

MR. SHU FU (*getting up, to the audience*): What do you think of me, ladies and gentlemen? Could anyone do more? Could anyone be less selfish? More farsighted? A small dinner! What vulgar and clumsy thoughts this would bring into the minds of most people. But nothing like that will happen. Nothing. She won't be touched. Not even casually. Not even accidentally while passing the salt! Nothing but ideas will be exchanged. Two souls will find each other over the flowers on the table, white chrysanthemums by the way. (*He makes a note of that.*) No, we won't exploit an unfortunate situation. We won't turn a disappointment to our advantage. Understanding and assistance will be offered. And almost without a sound. A single glance might perhaps acknowledge it. A glance which could also mean more.

MRS. SHIN: So everything went as you wished, Mr. Shu Fu?

MR. SHU FU: Oh, just as I wished! There'll presumably be a few changes in this district. A certain person has been shown the door and some of the plots against this shop will be spoiled. Certain people who still dare to harm the reputation of the chastest girl in this city will get into trouble with me in the future. What do you know about this Yang Sun?

MRS. SHIN: He's the dirtiest, laziest ...

MR. SHU FU: He's nothing. He doesn't exist. He can't be found, Mrs. Shin. (*Enter Sun.*)

SUN: What's going on here?

MRS. SHIN: Mr. Shu Fu, d'you want me to call Mr. Shui Ta? He won't want strangers loitering around in the store.

MR. SHU FU: Miss Shen Te is having an important talk with Mr. Shui Ta and mustn't be interrupted.

SUN: What, she's here? I didn't see her go in! What sort of a talk is that? I've got to be in on it!

MR. SHU FU (*preventing him from going into the back room*)**:** You'll have to be patient, my dear sir. I think I know who you are. Please take note that Miss Shen Te and I are about to announce our engagement.

SUN: What?

MRS. SHIN: That surprises you, doesn't it?

[*Sun is fighting with the barber to get into the backroom when Shen Te steps out of it.*]

MR. SHU FU: Excuse me, dear Shen Te. Perhaps you could explain ...

SUN: What's the matter, Shen Te? Are you crazy?

SHEN TE (*breathlessly*): Sun, my cousin and Mr. Shu Fu have come to an agreement: I'm to listen to Mr. Shu Fu's ideas about how to help the people of the neighborhood. (*pause*) My cousin wants to part us.

SUN: And you agree?

SHEN TE: Yes.

[*Pause.*]

SUN: Did they tell you I'm a bad man?

[*Shen Te is silent.*]

SUN: Maybe I am a bad man, Shen Te. And that's why I need you. I'm low. Without money, without manners. But I fight back. They're driving you into misfortune, Shen Te. (*He goes over to her and speaks in an undertone.*) Just look at him! Do you have no eyes in your head? (*With his hand on her shoulder*) Poor creature, now what did they want you to do? Make a reasonable match! Without me they'd just have sacrificed you. Admit that, but for me, you would have gone away with him!

SHEN TE: Yes.

SUN: A man you don't love.

SHEN TE: Yes.

SUN: Have you forgotten everything? How it was raining?

SHEN TE: No.

SUN: How you cut me from the tree? How you bought me a cup of water? How you promised me the money so I could fly again?

SHEN TE (*trembling*): What do you want?

SUN: I want you to come with me.

SHEN TE: Mr. Shu Fu, forgive me, I want to go away with Sun.

SUN: We're lovers, you know. (*He leads her to the door.*) Where is the key to the store? (*He takes it from her pocket and hands it to Mrs. Shin.*) Leave it outside the door when you're through. Come on, Shen Te.

MR. SHU FU: But this is rape! (*Shouting to the back*) Mr. Shui Ta!

SUN: Tell him not to shout so much in here.

SHEN TE: Please don't call my cousin, Mr. Shu Fu. He doesn't agree with me, I know. But he's not right, I can feel it. (*To the audience*)

I want to go with the one I love
I don't want to reckon what it will cost
I don't want to consider if it is wise
I want to go with the one I love.

SUN: That's it. (*Exeunt.*)

ACT 5-A

[Before the curtain. Shen Te, in her wedding outfit and on the way to her wedding, turns to the audience.]

SHEN TE: I've had a terrible experience. As I was stepping out of the house, gay and full of expectation, the carpet dealer's old wife was standing on the street. She was trembling all over, and she told me that her husband had fallen sick from excitement and worry about the money they'd lent me. She thought it best that I return the money to her now in any case. Of course I promised it to her. She was very relieved, wished me the best of luck with tears in her eyes and asked me to forgive her because she couldn't altogether trust my cousin, nor, unfortunately, Sun. I had to sit down when she'd gone, I was so alarmed by my own behavior. With my emotions in an uproar, I threw myself again into the arms of Yang Sun. I couldn't resist his voice and his caresses. The bad things he said to Shui Ta didn't teach Shen Te anything. Sinking into his arms, I thought: the gods wanted me to be good to myself too.

To let no one perish, not even one's self,
To fill everyone with happiness, even one's self,
That is good.

How could I simply forget those two good old people? Like a small hurricane. Sun just swept away my store and all my friends in the direction of Peking. But he's not bad and he loves me. As long as I'm with him, he won't do anything bad. What men say between themselves doesn't count. He just wants to seem big and powerful and above all hard-boiled. When I tell him that the old couple won't be able to pay their taxes, he'll understand everything. He'd rather go and work in the cement factory than owe his flying to a crime. Of course flying's a great passion with Sun. Shall I be strong enough to bring out the good in him? Now, on the way to my wedding, I waver between fear and joy. (*She goes quickly off*)

ACT 6

[*A side room of a cheap restaurant in the suburbs. A waiter pours out wine for the wedding party. Near Shen Te are the Grandfather, the Sister-in-law, the Niece, Mrs. Shin, and The Unemployed. In the corner, alone stands a Priest. Down stage, Sun is talking with his mother, Mrs. Yang. He is wearing a dinner jacket.*]

SUN: Something unpleasant. Mamma. She just told me in all innocence that she can't sell the store for me. Somebody or other is bringing a claim because they lent her the two hundred silver dollars which she gave to you. And her cousin said that there wasn't any written agreement.

MRS. YANG: What did you say to her? Of course you can't marry her now.

SUN: There's no sense in talking with her about these things. She's got a thick head. I've sent for her cousin.

MRS. YANG: But he wants to marry her to the barber.

SUN: I've put an end to that marriage. The barber's been insulted. Her cousin will soon understand that if I don't hand over the two hundred, the creditors will seize the store and the store will be gone, but if I don't get the three hundred, my job will be gone too.

MRS. YANG: I'll look for him outside the restaurant. Go to your bride, now. Sun!

SHEN TE (*pouring wine, to the audience*)**:** I wasn't mistaken in him. I couldn't see a trace of disappointment in his face. He's perfectly cheerful though it must be a heavy blow for him to have to give up flying. I love him very much. (*She waves Sun over.*) Sun, you haven't drunk a toast with the bride!

SUN: What shall we drink to?

SHEN TE: Let's drink to the future.

[*They drink.*]

SUN: When the bridegroom's tuxedo will no longer be borrowed!

SHEN TE: But when the bride's dress will still get rained on now and then.

SUN: To everything we wish for!

SHEN TE: That it may quickly come true!

MRS. YANG (*on the way out, to Mrs. Shin*)**:** I'm delighted with my son. I've always impressed it on him that he can get whoever he wants. Why, he's a trained mechanic and flier. And what does he tell me now? "I'm marrying for love. Mamma," he says, "money isn't everything." It's a love match! (*To the Sister-in-law*) It has to happen once, hasn't it? But it's hard for a mother, it's hard. (*Calling back to the Priest*) Don't cut it too short. If you take as much time for the ceremony as you took to haggle about the price, it'll be dignified all right. (*To Shen Te*) We've got to postpone things a little still, my dear. One of our most beloved guests hasn't arrived yet. (*To all*) Excuse me, please. (*Exit.*)

THE SISTER-IN-LAW: We'll gladly be patient as long as there's wine.

[*They all sit down.*]

THE UNEMPLOYED: We're not missing anything.

SUN (*loud and jokingly before the guests*)**:** And before the marriage I've still got to give you a little quiz. A not unnecessary thing when a wedding is held at such short notice. (*To the guests*) I've no idea what sort of a wife I'm getting. That worries me. (*To Shen Te*) For instance, can you make five cups of tea with three tea leaves?

SHEN TE: No.

SUN: I see I won't be getting any tea. Can you sleep on a sack of straw the size of the book the priest is reading?

SHEN TE: With someone else?

SUN: Alone.

SHEN TE: In that case, no.

SUN: I'm horrified at the wife I'm getting.

[*They all laugh. Behind Shen Te, Mrs. Yang steps into the doorway. With a shrug of her shoulders, she tells Sun that there's no sign of the expected guest.*]

MRS. YANG (*to the Priest, who has shown her his watch*)**:** Don't be in such a hurry. It can be a matter of minutes. I can see they're drinking and smoking and no one's in a hurry. (*She sits down by the guests.*)

SHEN TE: Don't we have to talk about how we're going to arrange everything?

MRS. YANG: Oh, please, let's not talk shop. Shoptalk introduces a common note into the celebration, doesn't it?

[*The entrance bell rings. They all look to the door but nobody enters.*]

SHEN TE: Who's your mother waiting for, Sun?

SUN: That's a surprise for you. By the way, how's your cousin Shui Ta? I got on with him. A very sensible man! What a brain! Why don't you say anything?

SHEN TE: I don't know. I don't want to think of him.

SUN: Why not?

SHEN TE: Because you shouldn't get on well with him. If you love me, you can't love him.

SUN: Then may the three devils fetch him: the Fog-devil, the Engine-trouble devil, and the Empty-gas-tank devil! Drink, you stubborn girl! (*He makes her drink.*)

THE SISTER-IN-LAW (*to Mrs. Shin*)**:** Something's wrong here.

MRS. SHIN: What else did you expect?

THE PRIEST (*resolutely stepping up to Mrs. Yang, a watch in his hand*)**:** I've got to go, Mrs. Yang. I've got another wedding to attend to, and tomorrow morning a funeral.

MRS. YANG: D'you think I like all this postponing? We were hoping to manage with one pitcher of wine. But look how it's coming to an end! (*Loudly to Shen Te*) My dear Shen Te, I can't understand where your cousin can be all this time!

SHEN TE: My cousin?

MRS. YANG: But, my dear, it's him we're waiting for! I'm just old fashioned enough to think that such a close relative of the bride should be present at the wedding.

SHEN TE: Oh Sun, is it because of the three hundred silver dollars?

SUN (*without looking at her*)**:** Can't you hear? She's old fashioned. Well, I'm considerate. We'll wait another fifteen minutes and if he hasn't come then because the three devils have got him, we'll start!

MRS. YANG: I guess you all know already that my son is getting a job as a mail pilot. I'm very pleased about it. In these times, we have to make good money.

THE SISTER-IN-LAW: It's to be in Peking, isn't it?

MRS. YANG: Yes, in Peking.

SHEN TE: You've got to tell your mother. Sun, that Peking is out of the question.

SUN: Your cousin will tell her, if he agrees with you. Between us: I don't agree.

SHEN TE (*appalled*)**:** Sun!

SUN: How I hate this Setzuan. What a town! Do you know what they all look like when I half close my eyes? Horses! They fret and screw their necks up: what's thundering there above them? How's that? They're no longer needed? What, their time's up already? Let them bite themselves to death in their horse town! O to get out of here!

SHEN TE: But I've promised the money to the old couple.

SUN: Yes, you told me. And since you do stupid things like that, it's lucky your cousin's coming. Drink, and leave business to us! We'll fix it up.

SHEN TE (*horrified*)**:** But my cousin can't come.

SUN: What do you mean?

SHEN TE: He can't come!

SUN: And how do you figure our future? Tell me that.

SHEN TE: I thought you still had the two hundred silver dollars. We could return them tomorrow and keep the tobacco, which is worth a lot more. Then we'll sell it together in front of the cement factory since we can't pay the half year's rent.

SUN: Forget it! Forget it fast, sister! I am to stand on the street and sell tobacco to cement workers, I, Yang Sun, the flier! I'd rather run through all two hundred in one night! I'd rather throw it in the river! And your cousin knows me! I've arranged it with him. He's to bring the three hundred to the wedding.

SHEN TE: My cousin can't come.

SUN: And I thought he couldn't stay away.

SHEN TE: He can't be where I am.

SUN: How mysterious!

SHEN TE: Sun, you've got to know it: he's not your friend. I'm the one that loves you. My cousin Shui Ta doesn't love anybody. He's my friend, but he's no friend to my friends. He was thinking of the job at Peking when he agreed to your getting the old couple's money. But he won't bring you the three hundred silver dollars to the wedding.

SUN: And why not?

SHEN TE (*looking into his eyes*)**:** He says you only bought one ticket to Peking. SUN: Yes, that was so yesterday, but just look what I can show him today! (*He pulls two pieces of paper halfway out of his breast pocket.*) The old woman needn't see. Here's two tickets to Peking. One for me and one for you. Do you still think your cousin's against the marriage?

SHEN TE: No. The job's good. And I don't have my store any more.

SUN: Because of you I sold our furniture.

SHEN TE: Don't go on! Don't show me the tickets! I'm too afraid I might simply go with you. But I can't give you the three hundred silver dollars. Sun. What's to become of the old couple?

SUN: And what's to become of me? (*pause*) Better drink some more! Or are you a cautious person? I don't want a cautious wife. If I drink, I'll fly again. And you, if you drink, you might possibly understand me.

SHEN TE: Don't think I don't understand you. You want to fly and I can't help you.

SUN: "Here's a plane, my darling, but it's only got one wing!"

SHEN TE: Sun, we can't get the job at Peking honestly. That's why I need the two

hundred silver dollars which you got from me. Give them to me now. Sun!

SUN: "Give them to me now, Sun!" What exactly are you talking about? Are you my wife or aren't you? You're betraying me, you know that, don't you? Luckily for both of us, things don't depend on you. Everything's arranged.

MRS. YANG (*icily*)**:** Sun, are you sure the bride's cousin is coming? Since he's still not here it might almost seem that he has something against this marriage.

SUN: What are you thinking of, Mamma? We're bosom friends! I'll open the door wide so he'll find us right away when he comes to be his friend Sun's best man. (*He goes to the door and kicks it open. Then he returns, staggering somewhat since he has already drunk too much, and sits down again beside Shen Te.*) We're waiting. Your cousin's got more sense than you. Love, he says wisely, goes with living! And, more important than that, he knows what it means to you: no more store and no marriage either!

[*Everyone is waiting.*]

MRS. YANG: Now!

[*Steps can be heard and everyone looks toward the door. But the steps pass.*]

MRS. SHIN: It's going to be a scandal. I can feel it. I can smell it. The bride is waiting for the wedding but the groom's waiting for her cousin.

SUN: The cousin's taking his time.

SHEN TE (*softly*)**:** Oh, Sun!

SUN: To sit here with the tickets in my pocket and next to me a fool who doesn't know arithmetic. I can foresee the day when you'll send the police to my house to get the two hundred silver dollars.

SHEN TE (*to the audience*)**:** He is bad and he wants me to be bad too. Here I am, I love him, and he waits for the cousin. But around me are the frail: the old woman with her sick husband, the poor who in the morning wait for their rice at my door, and an unknown man from Peking who is worried about his job. And they all protect me by trusting me.

SUN (*staring at the glass pitcher in which there is no wine left*)**:** The glass pitcher of wine is our clock. We're poor people and when the guests have drunk the wine, the clock's run down forever.

[*Mrs. Yang beckons him to be silent, for steps can again be heard.*]

THE WAITER (*entering*)**:** Do you want another pitcher of wine, Mrs. Yang?

MRS. YANG: No, I think we've got enough. Wine only makes you warm, doesn't it?

MRS. SHIN: It's expensive too, I'd say.

MRS. YANG: Drinking always makes me perspire.

THE WAITER: Might I ask, then, for a settlement of the bill?

MRS. YANG (*not hearing him*)**:** Ladies and gentlemen, I ask you to be patient a little longer, the cousin must be on his way. (*To the Waiter*) Don't spoil the festivities!

THE WAITER: I can't let you leave without settling the bill.

MRS. YANG: But I'm known here!

THE WAITER: Exactly.

MRS. YANG: It's outrageous, the service today. What d'you say to that, Sun?

THE PRIEST: I take my leave. (*He goes off, ponderously.*)

MRS. YANG (*desperately*)**:** Just stay where you are! The priest's coming back in a few minutes.

SUN: Never mind, Mamma. Ladies and gentlemen, since the priest's gone away, we can't keep you.

THE SISTER-IN-LAW: Come on, grandfather!

THE GRANDFATHER (*earnestly emptying his glass*)**:** To the bride!

THE NIECE (*to Shen Te*)**:** Don't hold it against him. He wants to be friendly. He likes you.

MRS. SHIN: What a disgrace!

[*All the guests go off.*]

SHEN TE: Shall I go too, Sun?

SUN: No, you'll wait. (*He drags her by her bridal ornaments, messing them up.*) Isn't it your wedding? I'm still waiting and the old woman's waiting too. She wants to see her falcon (*he points at himself*) in the clouds! However, I almost believe now that it'll be Saint Nevernever Day before she'll step to her door and see his plane thundering over her house. (*To the empty seats, as if the guests were still present*) Ladies and gentlemen, what's the matter with the conversation? Don't you like it here? The wedding, after all, is only postponed a bit because of the important guest who's expected and because the bride doesn't yet know the meaning of love. For your entertainment, I, the bridegroom, will sing you a song. (*He sings.*)

THE SONG OF SAINT NEVERNEVER DAY

On a certain day, as is very well known,
Everyone will cry "Hooray,
The poor woman's son is on the golden throne!"
And the day's Saint Nevernever Day.
On Saint Nevernever Day
He'll sit on the golden throne.

And on that day goodness will pay
And badness will cost you your head
And merit and gain will smile and play
While exchanging salt and bread.
On Saint Nevernever Day
While exchanging salt and bread.

And the grass will look down at the sky
And the pebbles will roll up the stream
And men will be good without batting an eye
They will make of our earth a dream.
On Saint Nevernever Day
They will make of our earth a dream.

And on that day I shall be a flier
And you'll be one of the best
And you, idle man, will have work at last
You, woman, will get your rest.
On Saint Nevernever Day
You, woman, will get your rest.

And because we can hardly wait for that time
All this will begin, I know,
Not at night, at seven or eight or nine,
But at the first cock crow.
On Saint Nevernever Day
At the very first cock crow.

MRS. YANG: He won't come now.

[*The three sit there, two of them looking toward the door.*]

ACT 6-A

[*Wang's sleeping quarters. Again the Gods appear to Wang in a dream. He has fallen asleep over a large book. Music.*]

WANG: I'm glad you've come, illustrious ones! Permit me a question which disturbs me deeply. In the ruined hut of a priest who has moved away to become a laborer in the cement factory, I found a book and in it a strange passage. I absolutely must read it to you. Here it is. (*With his left hand he turns the pages of an imaginary book above the real book which is lying in his lap. He lifts up the imaginary book to read from while the real book remains where it is.*) "In Sung there is a place called Thorngrove. Catalpas, cypresses, and mulberry trees grow there. Now trees which are one or two spans in circumference are cut down by those who want sticks to make dog kennels with. Those of three or four feet in circumference are cut down by rich families in search of boards for coffins. Those of seven or eight feet in circumference are cut down by people seeking beams for their luxury villas. Thus none of the trees lives its allotted span, for all perish before their time is up by saw and ax. Such are the tribulations of usefulness."

THE THIRD GOD: In that case the one men have least use for would be the best.

WANG: No, only the happiest. It's the worst but also the happiest.

THE FIRST GOD: The things people write!

THE SECOND GOD: Why does this parable affect you so deeply, water seller?

WANG: Because of Shen Te, illustrious one! She has come to grief in her love because she followed the commandment, love thy neighbor! Perhaps she is really too good for this world, illustrious ones!

THE FIRST GOD: Nonsense, weak and wretched man! Lice and doubts, it seems, have almost eaten you up.

WANG: Certainly, illustrious one, forgive me! I only thought you might be able to intervene.

THE FIRST GOD: That's quite impossible. Our friend here (*he points to the Third God who has a black eye*) intervened in a quarrel only yesterday. You can see the consequences.

WANG: But her cousin had to be called in again. He's an incredibly skillful man, as I found out for myself, but not even he could achieve anything. The store seems to be lost.

THE THIRD GOD (*a bit worried*)**:** Perhaps we should help after all?

THE FIRST GOD: I'm of the opinion that she should help herself.

THE SECOND GOD (*sternly*)**:** The worse the situation of a good man, the better he shows himself. Suffering ennobles!

THE FIRST GOD: All our hopes rest on her.

THE THIRD GOD: Things aren't what they might be with our search. Now and then we find some good beginnings, gratifying intentions, many high principles, but all that hardly constitutes a good human being. And when we do find halfway good people, they don't live in a dignified, human way. (*Confidentially*) Things are especially bad with our sleeping quarters. You can see where we spend the nights by the straw sticking to our clothes.

WANG: Just one thing, couldn't you at least ...

THE GODS: No. We're onlookers. We firmly believe that our good woman will find her own way on this dark earth. The heavier the burden the greater will be her strength! Just wait, water seller, and, you'll see, everything will come to a good ...

[*The figures of the Gods have grown paler, their voices softer, all the time. Now they disappear and their voices are no longer heard.*]

ACT 7

[*The yard behind Shen Te's tobacco store. On a cart there are a few house furnishings. Shen Te and Mrs. Shin are taking do the washing from the line.*]

MRS. SHIN: I can't understand why you don't fight for your store tooth and nail.

SHEN TE: What? I can't even pay the rent. The old couple's two hundred silver dollars have to be returned today but since I've given them to someone else, I'll have to sell my tobacco to Mrs. Mi Tzu.

MRS. SHIN: Everything's gone then. No husband, no tobacco, no place to stay! That's what happens when somebody wants to be better than other people. What are you going to live off now?

SHEN TE: I don't know. Perhaps I can earn a little by sorting tobacco.

MRS. SHIN: What are Mr. Shui Ta's pants doing here? He must have gone away from here naked!

SHEN TE: He's got another pair of trousers.

MRS. SHIN: I thought you said he'd gone for good? Why did he leave his pants behind?

SHEN TE: Perhaps he doesn't need them any more.

MRS. SHIN: Shall I pack them away?

SHEN TE: No.

[*Mr. Shu Fu comes running in.*]

MR. SHU FU: Don't say anything. I know all. You sacrificed your love and happiness so as not to ruin two old people who trusted you. It's not in vain that this neighborhood, this suspicious and malevolent neighborhood, calls you the Angel of the Suburbs. Your fiancé couldn't rise to your moral level, so you left him. And now you're closing your store, this little haven for so many! I can't let that pass. Morning after morning I watched from my doorstep the little crowd of wretched people in front of your store and you distributing rice with your own hands. Will that never happen again? Must the good woman of Setzuan perish? Oh, if only you'd permit me to assist you with your good works! No, don't say anything! I don't want any assurances. No avowals that you wish to accept my help! But here. (*He pulls out a checkbook and signs a check which he puts on her cart.*) I'm making out a blank check to you. You can fill it out as you wish, for any sum. And now I go, quietly and modestly, making no claims, on tiptoe, full of veneration, selflessly. (*Exit.*)

MRS. SHIN (*examining the check*)**:** You're saved! The likes of you are lucky: you always find some idiot. But now fall to! Fill it out for a thousand silver dollars and I'll take it to the bank before he comes to his senses.

SHEN TE: Put the washing basket on the cart. I can pay the laundry bill without the check.

MRS. SHIN: What? You don't want to take the check? It's a crime! Is it just because you think you'd have to marry him? Sheer madness! People like him want to be led by the nose! It's the greatest bliss they know. Or do you still want to hold on to your flier when Yellow Street and the whole neigh borhood know how badly he treated you?

SHEN TE: It all comes from poverty. (*To the audience*)

I saw him puff up his cheeks in his sleep.
They were bad cheeks.
But in the morning I held his coat against the light
and saw the walls through it.
When I heard his cunning laugh, I grew afraid.
But when I saw his shoes full of holes,
I loved him dearly.

MRS. SHIN: So you're defending him after everything that's happened. I've never seen anyone quite as crazy. (*Angrily*) I shall breathe more easily when we're rid of you in this neighborhood.

SHEN TE (*staggering while taking down the wash*)**:** I'm a bit dizzy.

MRS. SHIN (*taking the wash from her*)**:** Do you often get dizzy when you stretch or bend? If only there isn't a little visitor on the way! (*She laughs.*) What a pretty mess! If that's what's happened, it's all up with the big check! It wasn't meant for an occasion of that sort.

[*She goes to the back with a basket. Shen Te looks after her without moving. Then she looks at her body, feels it, and a great joy comes over her face.*]

SHEN TE (*softly*)**:** O joy! A human being is growing in my womb. Nothing can be seen yet. But he's there already. The world awaits him secretly. In the towns, people are saying: Someone's coming now who's got to be reckoned with. (*In pantomime she introduces her little son to the audience.*) A flier! Welcome a new conqueror of unknown mountains and unreachable regions! One who brings the mail from man to man over the unpassable deserts! (*She begins to walk up and down, leading her little son by the hand.*) Come, son, look at the world! Here, that's a tree. Bow to it, greet it. (*She shows him how to bow.*) That's it: now you know each other. Stop, here comes the water seller. A friend. Give him your hand. Don't be afraid. A glass of fresh water for my son, please. It's warm today. (*She gives him the glass.*) O dear, the policeman! We'll make a big circle around him. Perhaps we'll get a few cherries over there in the rich Mr. Feh Pung's garden. But we mustn't be seen there. Come, fatherless boy! You too want cherries! Easy, easy, son! (*They walk carefully, looking around.*) No, over here, the bushes will hide us. No, you can't go straight at them like that. (*He seems to pull her away. She resists.*) We've got to be reasonable. (*Suddenly she gives in.*) All right, if you really must go straight at them ... (*She lifts him up.*) Can you reach the cherries? Push them in your mouth, that's a safe place for them. (*She takes a cherry from him and puts it in her mouth.*) Tastes pretty good. O heavens, the policeman! Now we've got to run! (*They flee.*) There's the street. Quiet now, we'll walk slowly so we won't be noticed. As

if not the least thing had happened. (*She sings, walking along with the child.*)
For no reason a plum
Attacked a bum.
But the man, very quick,
Bit the plum in the neck.

[*Wang, the water seller, has come in, leading a child by the hand. He watches Shen Te with wonder. Wang coughs.*]

SHEN TE: Oh, Wang! Hello.

WANG: Shen Te, I've heard you're not so well off. You even had to sell your store to pay your debts. But here's a child without a roof over his head. He was running about in the stockyards. He seems to be one of Lin To's children. You remember the carpenter? He lost his shop a few weeks ago and has been drinking ever since. His children go hungry and hang around the streets. What can be done for them?

SHEN TE (*taking the child from him*): Come, little man! (*To the audience*)
You there! Someone is asking for shelter.
A bit of tomorrow is asking for today!
His friend, the conqueror, whom you know,
Is his advocate.
(*To Wang*) He can easily live in Mr. Shu Fu's cabins where I also may be going. I'm to have a baby too. But don't tell anyone or Yang Sun will hear it, and we'd only be in his way. Look for Mr. Lin To downtown, and tell him to come here.

WANG: Thanks a lot, Shen Te. I knew you'd find something. (*To the child*) You see, someone who's good always knows a way out. I'll run quickly and get your father. (*He starts to go.*)

SHEN TE: Oh Wang, now it comes back to me: how's your hand? I wanted to take the oath for you but my cousin ...

WANG: Don't worry about my hand. Look, I've already learned to get along without my right hand. I hardly need it any more. (*He shows her how he can handle his pole without using his right hand.*) Watch how I do it!

SHEN TE: But it mustn't grow stiff! There, take the cart, sell everything, and go to the doctor with the money. I'm ashamed to have let you down like this. And what will you think of my accepting the cabins from the barber?

WANG: The homeless can live there now. And so can you. That's more important than my hand. Now I'm going to get the carpenter. (*Exit.*)

SHEN TE: Promise me you'll go to the doctor!

[*Mrs. Shin has returned and has been waving to her.*]

MRS. SHIN: Are you crazy? Giving away the cart with your very last possessions! What's his hand to you? If the barber hears of it, he'll chase you out of the only shelter you can get. You haven't paid me for the laundry!

SHEN TE: Why are you so bad?

You tread on your fellow man.
Isn't it a strain?
Your veins swell with your efforts to be greedy.
Extended naturally, a hand gives and receives with equal ease.
Grabbing greedily, it has to strain. Alas!
What an enticement, to give! How pleasant, to be kind!
A good word slips out like a sigh of contentment.

[*Mrs. Shin goes angrily off.*]

SHEN TE (*to the child*)**:** Sit down here and wait till your father comes.

[*The child sits on the ground. Enter the Husband and Wife who came to live with Shen. Te on the day her store opened. They are dragging large sacks.*]

THE WIFE: Are you alone, Shen Te? (*Since Shen Te nods, she calls in her Nephew who is also carrying a sack.*) Where's your cousin?

SHEN TE: He's gone away.

THE WIFE: And is he coming back?

SHEN TE: No. I'm giving up the store.

THE WIFE: We know that. That's why we came. We've got a few sacks of raw tobacco here which someone owed us and we'd like to ask you to move them to your new home together with your belongings. We haven't got a place yet to take them to and we'd be so noticeable on the street. I don't see how you can deny us this small favor after all the trouble we got into in your store.

SHEN TE: I'll gladly do you the favor.

THE HUSBAND: And if someone should ask whose sacks these are, you can say they're yours.

SHEN TE: Who should ask me?

THE WIFE (*looking at her sharply*)**:** The police, for instance. They are prejudiced against us and want to ruin us. Where should we put the sacks?

SHEN TE: I don't know, just now I'd 'rather not do anything that might get me in jail.

THE WIFE: That's just like you. We're to lose the few miserable sacks of tobacco too, the only things we saved!

[*Shen Te maintains a stubborn silence.*]

THE HUSBAND: Just think, this tobacco could start us in the manufacturing business. We could go a long way!

SHEN TE: All right, I'll keep the sacks for you. For the time being, we'll put them in the back room.

[*She goes in with them. The child looks after her. Then, shyly glancing about, he goes to the garbage can and fishes around in it. He starts to eat out of it Shen Te and the others come back.*]

THE WIFE: You understand, I guess, that we depend on you completely.

SHEN TE: Yes. (*She sees the child and grows rigid.*)

THE HUSBAND: We'll look for you the day after tomorrow in Mr. Shu Fu's cabins.

SHEN TE: Go now, quickly. I'm not well.

[*She pushes them off. Exeunt the three.*]

SHEN TE: He is hungry. He's fishing in the garbage can. (*She picks up the child and, in the following speech, expresses her horror at the fate of poor children. She shows the audience the little gray mouth. She asserts her determination under no circumstances to treat her own child with such cruelty. During her speech the musicians start playing "The Song of the Defenselessness of the Gods and Good Men."*)

O son! O flier! Into what a world will you come?
They want to let you fish in the garbage can, even you!
Only look at the little gray mouth!
(*She shows the child to the audience.*)
How do you treat your offspring?
Have you no mercy on the fruit of your womb?
No pity for yourselves, unhappy men?
I shall defend my own even if I have to be a tigress to do it!
Having seen this, from now on, I divorce myself from everybody!
I will not rest till I have saved my son, if only him!
What I have learned in my school, the gutter,
With fisticuffs and deceit,

Will now be of use to you, my son!
I will be good to you, and a tigress, a wild beast
To all others,
If I have to.
And I shall have to.

[*She goes off to change into the cousin's clothes.*]

SHEN TE (*going*): Once more it has to be. The last time, I hope.

[*She has taken with her Shui Ta's trousers. The returning Mrs. Shin looks after her curiously. Enter the Sister-in-Jaw and the Grandfather. The music continues softly.*]

THE SISTER-IN-LAW: The store's closed. The furniture's in the yard. That's the end.

MRS. SHIN: The results of frivolity, sensuality, and self-love. And where's the journey to? Down, down, down! Into Mr. Shu Fu's cabins. With you.

THE SISTER-IN-LAW: She'll have a nice surprise! We've come to complain! Damp rat holes with rotten floors! The barber only offered them to us be cause his soap supplies got moldy there. "I have shelter for you, what do you say to that?" Shame! we say to that!

[*Enter the Unemployed*]

THE UNEMPLOYED: Is it true, Shen Te's moving away?

THE SISTER-IN-LAW: Yes, she wanted to sneak off. No one was supposed to find out.

MRS. SHIN: She's ashamed because she's ruined.

THE UNEMPLOYED (*excitedly*): She's got to call her cousin! Advise her to call her cousin! He's the only one who can still do something.

THE SISTER-IN-LAW: That's true. He's stingy enough but at least he'll save her store and then she'll help us again.

IBE UNEMPLOYED: I wasn't thinking of us, I was thinking of her. But, you're right, she should call him for our sake too.

[*Enter Wang with the Carpenter. He leads two children by the hand.*]

THE CARPENTER: I really can't thank you enough. (*To the others*) We're getting a place to live.

MRS. SHIN: Where?

THE CARPENTER: Mr. Shu Fu's cabins! And it was little Feng who brought the change about! (*He sees Feng.*) Well, here you are! "Here is someone asking for shelter," Miss Shen Te is supposed to have said, and at once she got us a place to stay. (*To the two children*) Thank your brother, you two! (*The Carpenter and his children gaily bow to the child.*) Our thanks, little friend!

[*Shui Ta has entered.*]

SHUI TA: May I ask what you all want here?

THE UNEMPLOYED: Mr. Shui Ta!

WANG: Good day, Mr. Shui Ta. I didn't know you'd come back. You know the carpenter, Mr. Lin To. Miss Shen Te has promised him a place in Mr. Shu Fu's cabins.

SHUI TA: Mr. Shu Fu's cabins are not available.

THE CARPENTER: So we can't live there?

SHUI TA: The space is reserved for something else.

THE SISTER-IN-LAW: Does that mean we have to get out too?

SHUI TA: I'm afraid so.

THE SISTER-IN-LAW: But where are we all to go?

SHUI TA (*shrugging his shoulders*)**:** As I understand Miss Shen Te, who has gone on a journey, it is not her intention to withdraw her aid completely. However, in the future, things will be ordered a bit more reasonably. No more food without services rendered in return. Instead, everyone will be given the opportunity to work himself up in an honest way. Miss Shen Te has decided to give you all work. Those of you who want to follow me now into Shu Fu's cabins will not be led into nothingness.

THE SISTER-IN-LAW: Does that mean we're all supposed to work for Shen Te now?

SHUI TA: Yes. You'll be making tobacco. In the room inside are three bales of goods. Get them!

THE SISTER-IN-LAW: Don't forget we owned a store once. We prefer to work for ourselves. We have our own tobacco.

SHUI TA (*to the Unemployed and the Carpenter*)**:** Perhaps you will want to work for Shen Te since you don't have your own tobacco.

[*The Carpenter and the Unemployed go in dejectedly. The Landlady enters.*]

THE LANDLADY: Well, Mr. Shui Ta, how're things with the sale? Here I have three hundred silver dollars.

SHUI TA: Mrs. Mi Tzu, I've decided not to sell, but to sign the lease.

THE LANDLADY: What? All of a sudden you don't need the money for the flier?

SHUI TA: No.

THE LANDLADY: And do you have the rent?

SHUI TA (*taking the barber's check from the cart and filling it out*)**:** Here I have a check for ten thousand silver dollars, made out by Mr. Shu Fu, who's interested in my cousin. Mrs. Mi Tzu, look for yourself. The two hundred silver dollars for the next half year's rent will be in your hands before 6 P.M..

And now, Mrs. Mi Tzu, allow me to continue my work. I'm very busy today and have to ask your pardon.

THE LANDLADY: Oh I see, Mr. Shu Fu steps into the flier's shoes! Ten thousand silver dollars! Nevertheless, Mr. Shui Ta, the young girls of today surprise me. They are fickle. And superficial too.

[*She goes out. The Carpenter and the Unemployed drag in the sacks.*]

THE CARPENTER: I don't know why I'm dragging your sacks.

SHUI TA: It's enough that I know. Your son here has a healthy appetite. He wants to eat, Mr. Lin To.

THE SISTER-IN-LAW (*seeing the sacks*)**:** Has my brother-in-law been here?

MRS. SHIN: Yes.

THE SISTER-IN-LAW: I thought so. I know these sacks. That's our tobacco!

SHUI TA: You better not say that so loud. This is my tobacco, as you can see from the fact that it was standing in my room. If you have any doubts, we can go to the police and remove them. Is that what you want?

THE SISTER-IN-LAW (*angrily*)**:** No.

SHUI TA: It seems you don't have tobacco of your own after all. Under these circumstances you will perhaps grasp the saving hand which Miss Shen Te is holding out to you? Be so kind now as to show me the way to Mr. Shu Fu's cabins.

[*Taking the Carpenter's youngest child by the hand, Shui Ta goes off, followed by the Carpenter, his other children, the Sister-in-law, the Grandfather, and the Unemployed. The Sister-in-law, the Carpenter, and the Unemployed drag the sacks.*]

WANG: He's a bad man. But Shen Te is good.

MRS. SHIN: I don't know. A pair of pants is missing from the clothes line and her cousin's wearing them. That must mean something. I'd like to know what.

[*Enter the old couple.*]

THE OLD WOMAN: Isn't Miss Shen Te here?

MRS. SHIN (*absent-mindedly*)**:** Gone away

THE OLD WOMAN: That's strange. She was going to bring us something.

WANG (*sadly looking at his hand*)**:** She was going to help me too. My hand's getting all stiff. I'm sure she'll be back soon. The cousin has never stayed long.

MRS. SHIN: He hasn't, has he?

ACT 7-A

[*Wang's sleeping quarters. Music. In his dream, the water seller tells the Gods his fears. The Gods are still on their long journey. They seem tired Stopping for a moment, they look over their shoulders toward the water seller.*]

WANG: Before your sudden appearance woke me, illustrious ones, I was dreaming. I saw my dear sister Shen Te in great distress in the rushes by the river at the place where those who commit suicide are found. She was staggering strangely and held her head low as if she were dragging something soft but heavy which was pulling her down in the mud. When I called to her, she told me she had to take the package of rules to the other shore without getting it wet since that would wipe away the writing. Actually I couldn't see that she was carrying anything. But I remembered with fear that you, the gods, had spoken to her about the great virtues, in gratitude for her taking you in when you were hard put to it for sleeping quarters, o shame! I'm sure you'll understand my worries.

THE THIRD GOD: What do you propose?

WANG: Somewhat fewer rules, illustrious ones! A little relaxation of the book of rules, benevolent ones, in view of the bad times.

THE THIRD GOD: As for instance, Wang, as for instance?

WANG: As for instance that only goodwill be required, instead of love, or ...

THE THIRD GOD: But that would be even more difficult, unhappy one!

WANG: Or fairness instead of justice.

THE THIRD GOD: But that would mean more work! WANG: Then just propriety instead of honor.

THE THIRD GOD: But, don't you see, that would mean more work, not less, you skeptic! (*Tired, they wander on.*)

ACT 8

[*Shui Ta's tobacco factory. Shui Ta has established a small tobacco factory in Mr. Shu Fu's cabins. Behind bars, fearfully dose together, are several families, especially women and children. Among them are the Sister-in-law, the Grandfather, the Carpenter, and his children. Enter Mrs. Yang followed by Yang Sun.*]

MRS. YANG (*to the audience*)**:** I have to tell you how the wisdom and strength of the universally respected Mr. Shui Ta has transformed my son Yang Sun from a depraved scamp into a useful person. As the whole neighborhood found out, Mr. Shui Ta opened a small but soon flourishing tobacco factory near the cattle runs. Three months ago I found it necessary to visit him there with my son. After a short time he received me.

[*Shui Ta comes out of the factory and goes to Mrs. Yang.*]

SHUI TA: How can I help you, Mrs. Yang?

MRS. YANG: Mr. Shui Ta, I'd like to put in a word for my son. This morning the police were at our house and we were told that you have brought an action in the name of Miss Shen Te for breach of promise of marriage. You also claim that Sun dishonestly got his hands on two hundred silver dollars.

SHUI TA: Quite right, Mrs. Yang.

MRS. YANG: Mr. Shui Ta, for the sake of the gods, couldn't you be merciful once more? The money's gone. He ran through it in two days when nothing came of the flying job. I know he's a good-for-nothing. He'd already sold my furniture and wanted to go to Peking without his old Mamma. (*She weeps.*) Miss Shen Te thought very highly of him once.

SHUI TA: What do you have to say, Mr. Yang Sun?

SUN (*darkly*)**:** The money's gone.

SHUI TA: Mrs. Yang, because of my cousin's incomprehensible weakness for your depraved son, I'm prepared to give him another chance. She told me that she expected honest work to produce an improvement. He can have a job in my factory. We will deduct the two hundred silver dollars from his salary bit by bit.

SUN: Then it's the factory or the jail?

SHUI TA: Take your choice.

SUN: And I guess I can't talk with Shen Te?

SHUI TA: No.

SUN: Where's my place?

MRS. YANG: A thousand thanks, Mr. Shui Ta! You are infinitely kind. The gods will reward you. (*To Sun*) You've departed from the right path. Now try your hand at honest work till you can face your mother again!

[*Sun follows Shui Ta into the factory. Mrs. Yang returns to the footlights.*]

MRS. YANG: The first weeks were hard for Sun. The work didn't agree with him. He had little opportunity to distinguish himself. But in the third week a small incident came to his aid.

[*Sun and the former Carpenter Lin To are each dragging two bales of tobacco.*]

THE CARPENTER (*he stops, groaning, and sits down on a bale*)**:** I can hardly go on. I'm not young enough for this work.

SUN (*sitting down too*)**:** Why don't you just throw the sacks in their faces?

THE CARPENTER: And how're we to live? To get a bare living I've even got to use the children. If Miss Shen Te could see this! She was good.

SUN: She was all right. If conditions hadn't been so lousy, we could have made out quite nicely together. I'd like to know where she is. We better go on. He usually comes about this time.

[*They get up. Sun sees Shui Ta approaching.*]

SUN: Give me one of your sacks, you cripple! (*Sun takes one of the bales from Lin To.*)

THE CARPENTER: Thanks a lot! Now if she were here and saw how you help an old man you'd soon be in favor. Oh dear!

[*Enter Shui Ta.*]

MRS. YANG: And of course Mr. Shui Ta saw right away what it means to be a good worker not shrinking from any job. And he stepped in.

SHUI TA: Stop, you! What's going on? Are you only carrying one sack?

THE CARPENTER: I'm a bit tired today, Mr. Shui Ta, and Yang Sun was kind enough to ...

SHUI TA: You're going back to take three bales, my friend. What Yang Sun can do, you can do. Yang Sun has the right attitude and you have not.

MRS. YANG (*while the former Carpenter gets two more bales*)**:** Of course, not a word to Sun but Mr. Shui Ta was wise to the situation. And the following Saturday when the wages were being paid out ...

[*A table is brought in and Shui Ta arrives with a bag of money. Standing Next to the foreman—the former Unemployed—he pays the wages. Sun steps up to the table.*]

THE UNEMPLOYED: Yang Sun, six silver dollars.

SUN: Excuse me, it can't be more than five. Only five silver dollars. (*He takes the list held by the foreman.*) Please look, here are marked six working days. That's a mistake. I was absent one day because of some court business. (*Hypocritically*) I don't want to get anything I don't deserve, however lousy the pay is!

THE UNEMPLOYED: Okay, five silver dollars! (*To Shui Ta*) A rare case, Mr. Shui Ta!

SHUI TA: How can it say six days here if it was only five?

THE UNEMPLOYED: I must have made a mistake, Mr. Shui Ta. (*To Sun, coldly*) It won't happen again.

SHUI TA (*calling Sun aside*)**:** I noticed the other day that you're a strong man and don't hold your strength back. You give it to the firm. Today I see you're even honest. Does it often happen that the foreman makes mistakes in favor of the employees?

SUN: He's got friends among the workers and they look on him as one of themselves.

SHUI TA: I see. Well, one good turn deserves another. Would you like some little recompense?

SUN: No. But perhaps I may point to the fact that I'm also intelligent. I've had an education, you know. The foreman means well enough by the workers but he's uneducated and can't understand what the firm needs. Give me a trial period of one week, Mr. Shui Ta, and I think I'll be able to prove to you that my intelligence can be worth more to the firm than my physical strength.

MRS. YANG: Those were daring words, but that evening I said to my son: You're a flier. Show that, even where you are now, you can rise! Fly, my falcon! And, really, education and intelligence can do great things! How can you belong to the better sort of people without them? My son worked rue miracles in Mr. Shui Ta's factory!

[*Sun stands with his legs apart behind the workers. Above their heads is a basket of raw tobacco which they are handing along.*]

SUN: You there, I don't call that honest work! This basket has got to move faster! (*To a child*) Sit on the floor where you don't take up so much room! And you, yes you over there, you can easily take on the pressing too! Lazy dogs, what're you getting paid for? Hurry up with the basket! The devil! Put grandfather on one side and let him pick with the children! No more laziness now! To my beat, the whole thing!

[*He claps the rhythm with his hands and the basket moves faster.*]

MRS. YANG: And no enmity, no abuse from uneducated people—and there was plenty of it—could stop my son from doing his duty.

[*One of the workers starts The Song of the Eighth Elephant. The others join in the refrain.*]

THE SONG OF THE EIGHTH ELEPHANT

Seven elephants had Mr. Dschin
And then there was Number Eight.
Seven were wild. Number Eight was tame
Number Eight guarded the gate.
Run faster!
Mr. Dschin has a forest park
It must be cleared before nightfall
And now it will soon be dark!

Seven elephants were clearing the forest
Mr. Dschin rode Number Eight.
And when the seven toiled all day
Number Eight would quietly wait.
Dig faster!
Mr. Dschin has a forest park
It must be cleared before nightfall
And now it will soon be dark!

Seven elephants had had enough
Of felling trees each day till late.
Mr. Dschin was angry at the seven, but he
Gave a bushel of rice to Number Eight.
What does it mean?

Mr. Dschin has a forest park
It must be cleared before nightfall
And now it will soon be dark!

Seven elephants they hadn't a tusk
Number Eight had a tusk which he used.
And when Number Eight cut the other seven up
Mr. Dschin stood there and was amused.
Keep on digging!
Mr. Dschin has a forest park
It must be cleared before nightfall
And now it will soon be dark!

[*Smoking a cigar, Shui Ta has come casually strolling forward Yang Sun, laughing, has joined in the refrain of the third stanza and speeded up the tempo of the last by clapping his hands.*]

MRS. YANG: We really can't thank Mr. Shui Ta enough. Almost without lifting a finger, with wisdom and strength alone, he's brought out all the good that lay hidden in Sun. He didn't make him fantastic promises like his cousin whom they praise so highly. He just forced him into honest work. Today, Sun is quite a different person. You'll have to admit that! A noble man is like a bell. If you ring it, it rings, and if you don't, it don't, as the saying goes.

ACT

[Shen Te's tobacco store. The store has become an office with club chairs and fine carpets. It is raining. Shui Ta, now fat, is sending away the Old Man and his wife. Mrs. Shin, amused, looks on. She is obviously in new clothes.]

SHUI TA: I'm sorry I can't tell you when she'll be back.

THE OLD WOMAN: We got a letter today with the two hundred silver dollars which we once lent her. It had no return address. But the letter must have come from Shen Te. We'd like to write to her. What's her address?

SHUI TA: I'm sorry I don't know that either.

THE OLD MAN: Let's go.

THE OLD WOMAN: She's got to come back sometime.

[Shui Ta bows. The two old people go off, uncertain and worried.]

MRS. SHIN: They got their money too late. Now they've lost their store because they couldn't pay their taxes.

SHUI TA: Why didn't they come to me?

MRS. SHIN: People don't like to come to you. At first, I guess, they were waiting for Shen Te to come back, because they had nothing in writing. Then at the critical moment the old man got a fever and his wife stayed with him day and night.

SHUI TA (*he has to sit down; he is beginning to feel sick*)**:** I'm dizzy again.

MRS. SHIN (*attending to him*)**:** You're in your seventh month! The excitement isn't good for you. You can be glad you've got me. No one can get along without help from others. Well, I'll be at your side when your hardest hour comes. (*She laughs.*)

SHUI TA (*weakly*)**:** Can I count on it, Mrs. Shin?

MRS. SHIN: I'll say. Of course it'll cost you a bit. Open your collar, you'll feel better.

SHUI TA (*wretchedly*)**:** It's all for the child's sake, Mrs. Shin.

MRS. SHIN: All for the child.

SHUI TA: I'm getting fat too fast. It must draw attention.

MRS. SHIN: They put it down to your wealth.

SHUI TA: And what'll happen to the little one?

MRS. SHIN: You ask that three times a day. It'll be taken care of. It'll have the best that money can buy.

SHUI TA: Yes. (*anxiously*) And it must never see Shui Ta.

MRS. SHIN: Never. Always Shen Te.

SHUI TA: But the rumors in the neighborhood! The things the water seller says! The store is watched!

MRS. SHIN: As long as the barber doesn't know anything, nothing's lost. Drink some of this water.

[*Enter Sun in a smart suit and with a businessman's brief case. He looks surprised at finding Shui Ta in Mrs. Shin's arms.*]

SUN: I guess I'm intruding.

SHUI TA (*getting up with difficulty and going to the door, staggering*)**:** Until tomorrow, Mrs. Shin!

[*Mrs. Shin, putting on her gloves, smiles and goes off.*]

SUN: Gloves! Where from, what for, and how? Is she fleecing you maybe? (*Since Shui Ta does not answer*) Are even you susceptible to the tender emotions? Funny. (*He takes a sheet of paper out of his brief case.*) Anyway, you haven't been at your best, lately, not as you used to be. Moods. Indecisions. Are you ill? The business suffers. Here's another letter from the police. They want to close the factory. They say that at the very most they can only permit twice the lawful number of workers. You've got to do something now, Mr. Shui Ta.

[*Shui Ta looks at him absent-mindedly for a moment. Then he goes into the backroom and returns with a bag. He pulls out a new bowler hat and throws it on the desk.*]

SHUI TA: The firm wishes representatives to be decently dressed.
SUN: Did you buy that for me?
SHUI TA (*indifferently*): Try it on and see if it fits.

[*Sun is surprised but puts it on. Shui Ta looks him over and puts the bow in place.*]

SUN: Your servant! But don't evade me again! You've got to discuss the new project with the barber today.
SHUI TA: The barber's demanding impossible conditions.
SUN: Of what kind? If only you'd tell me.
SHUI TA (*evasively*): The cabins are good enough.
SUN: Yes, good enough for the rabble working there. But not good enough for the tobacco. It gets damp. Before the meeting I'll have a talk with Mrs. Mi Tzu about her buildings. If we have them, we can fire this bunch of beggars, abortions, and walking scarecrows. They're not good enough. We'll have a cup of tea, I'll stroke Mrs. Mi Tzu's fat knees, and we'll get her buildings half price.
SHUI TA (*sharply*): No. In the interest of the firm's reputation, I want your behavior always to be personally reserved and coolly businesslike.
SUN: Why are you so irritated? Are those unpleasant rumors bothering you?
SHUI TA: I don't pay any attention to rumors.
SUN: Then it must be the rain again. Rain always makes you irritable and

melancholy. I'd like to know why.

WANG'S VOICE (*from outside*):

I'm selling water, water,
As I stand here in the rain. For such a little water
I've suffered too much pain. And now I shout: "Buy water!"
But no one's buying
Parched and dying
And drinking and paying ...

SUN: Here's that damned water seller. He'll be starting his heckling again.

WANG'S VOICE (*from outside*): Aren't there any good people left in the city of Setzuan? Not even here on the square where the good Shen Te used to live? Where is she who even when it was raining bought a little water from me in the gladness of her heart many months ago? Where is she now? Has no one seen her? Has no one heard from her? She went into this house one evening and never came out again.

SUN: Shall I shut his trap for him? What's it to him where she is? By the way, I think you're only keeping it secret so that I won't find out.

WANG (*entering*): Mr. Shui Ta, I'm asking you again when Shen Te will come back. It's six months now since she went away. (*Shui Ta is silent.*) In the meantime much has happened which she would never have put up with. (*Shui Ta is still silent.*) Mr. Shui Ta, there are rumors in the district that something must have happened to Shen Te. We, her friends, are very worried. Have the goodness to give us her address!

SHUI TA: Unfortunately, I'm not free at the moment, Mr. Wang. Come back next week.

WANG (*excitedly*): In the mornings there used to be rice at her door. For the needy. It has been there again lately!

SHUI TA: And what do people conclude from this?

WANG: That Shen Te hasn't gone away at all, but ...

SHUI TA: But what? (*Wang is silent.*) Then I'll give you my answer. And it is final. If you're Shen Te's friend, Mr. Wang, ask about her as little as possible. That's my advice.

WANG: Nice advice! Mr. Shui Ta, Shen Te told me before her disappearance that she was pregnant!

SUN: What?

SHUI TA (*quickly*)**:** It's a lie!

WANG (*very earnestly to Shui Ta*)**:** Mr. Shui Ta, you mustn't believe that Shen Te's friends will stop asking about her. A good person isn't so easily forgotten. There aren't many. (*Exit.*)

[*Motionless Shui Ta looks after him, then goes quickly into the back room.*]

SUN (*to the audience*)**:** Shen Te pregnant! I'm beside myself! I've been swindled! She must have told her cousin right away and that scoundrel sent her away immediately! "Pack your suitcase and disappear before the child's father gets wind of it." It's absolutely unnatural. It's inhuman. I have a son, a Yang appears on the scene, and what happens? The girl disappears and I'm left here to slave! (*He gets angry.*) I'm put off with a hat! (*He stamps on it.*) Criminal! Thief! Kidnapper! And the girl's virtually without a protector! (*Sobbing can be heard from the back room. He stands still.*) Did I hear sobbing? Who is it? It's stopped. What sobs are these? That cunning dog Shui Ta doesn't sob! Who sobs then? And what does it mean that the rice is said to be at the door in the mornings? Is the girl here after all? Is he just hiding her? Who else could be sobbing? That would be just the thing I want! If she's pregnant I've got to find her!

[*Shui Ta returns from the back room. He goes to the door and looks out into the rain.*]

SUN: Well, where is she?

SHUI TA (*putting up his hand and listening*)**:** Just a moment! It's nine o'clock. But one can't hear a thing today. The rain's too heavy.

SUN (*ironically*)**:** And what do you want to hear?

SHUI TA: The mail plane.

SUN: Stop fooling.

SHUI TA: I was once told that you wanted to fly? Have you lost that desire?

SUN: I'm not complaining about my present position, if that's what you mean. I don't care for night work, you know. Flying the mail is night work. The firm's become very dear to me, so to speak. It is after all the firm of my one time future wife, even if she has gone away. And she has, hasn't she?

SHUI TA: Why do you ask?

SUN: Maybe because her affairs still don't leave me altogether unmoved.

SHUI TA: That might interest my cousin.

SUN: In any case. I'm still sufficiently concerned in her affairs not to close my eyes if, for instance, she were kept under lock and key.

SHUI TA: By whom?

SUN: By you!

[*Pause*]

SHUI TA: What would you do?

SUN: I might, to begin with, start arguing about my position in the firm.

SHUI TA: Oh, I see. And if the firm, that is, if I should give you an adequate position, could I count on your giving up all further investigations concerning your one-time future wife?

SUN: Perhaps.

SHUI TA: And what sort of new position are you thinking of?

SUN: The top one. I'd be thinking of throwing you out, for example.

SHUI TA: And if, instead of me, the firm threw you out?

SUN: I'd probably come back. And not alone.

SHUI TA: But?

SUN: With the police.

SHUI TA: With the police. And suppose the police found no one here?

SUN: Then I suppose they'd search this back room. Mr. Shui Ta, my longing for the lady of my heart is insatiable. I feel I must do something in order to fold her in my arms again. (*Calmly*) She's pregnant and needs someone around. I've got to talk it over with the water seller. (*He goes.*)

[*Shui Ta looks after him without moving. Then he quickly returns to the back room. He brings out various belongings of Shen Te's, underwear, dresses, toilet articles. He looks a long time at the shawl which Shen Te bought from the Old Man and his wife. He then makes all these things up into a bundle and, hearing a noise, hides it under the table. Enter the Landlady and Mr. Shu Fu. They greet Shui Ta and put away their umbrellas and rubbers.*]

THE LANDLADY: Fall's coming on, Mr. Shui Ta.

MR. SHU FU: A sad season!

THE LANDLADY: And where's your charming secretary? A terrible lady-killer! But I guess you don't know that side of him. All the same he knows how to combine charm with attention to business in a way which can only be to your advantage.

SHUI TA (*bowing*): Won't you take a seat?

[*They sit down and start smoking.*]

SHUI TA: My friends, an unforeseen incident which might have certain conse quences forces me to speed up the negotiations. Negotiations concerning the future of the project I've been working on: Mr. Shu Fu, my factory is in difficulties.

MR. SHU FU: It always is.

SHUI TA: But now the police are openly threatening to close it if I can't point to negotiations for a new project. Mr. Shu Fu, it's a question of my cousin's one piece of property. Now you've always displayed the liveliest interest in my cousin.

MR. SHU FU: Mr. Shui Ta, I have a deep aversion to talking about your constantly expanding projects. I speak about a small dinner with your cousin; you hint at financial difficulties. I put cabins for the homeless at your cousin's disposal; you establish a factory there. I hand her a check; you present it. Your cousin disappears; you ask for ten thousand silver dollars, remarking that my cab ins are too small. Sir, where is your cousin?

SHUI TA: Mr. Shu Fu, don't worry. I can inform you today that she'll be back very soon.

MR. SHU FU: Soon? When? You've been saying "soon" for weeks.

SHUI TA: I'm not demanding new signatures from you. I've merely asked whether you'd show more interest in my project if my cousin returned.

MR. SHU FU: I've told you a thousand times that I'm ready to discuss everything with your cousin and nothing with you. However, it seems that you want to put obstacles in the way of such a discussion.

SHUI TA: Not any more.

MR. SHU FU: When will it take place then?

SHUI TA (*uncertainly*)**:** In three months.

MR. SHU FU (*annoyed*)**:** Then I'll sign in three months.

SHUI TA: But everything has to be prepared.

MR. SHU FU: You can prepare everything, Shui Ta, if you're convinced that your cousin will really come at this time.

SHUI TA: Mrs. Mi Tzu, are you, for your part, ready to confirm to the police that I may have your workrooms?

THE LANDLADY: Certainly, if you'll let me have your secretary. You've known for weeks that's my condition. (*To Mr. Shu Fu*) The young man's so efficient in business and I need a manager.

SHUI TA: You've got to understand that I can't do without Mr. Yang Sun just now, with all the difficulties I'm having. And my health has been failing me lately. I was ready from the beginning to let you have him, but ...

THE LANDLADY: Yes, but?

[*Pause*]

SHUI TA: All right, he'll call on you tomorrow, in your office.

MR. SHU FU: I am very glad that you were able to reach this decision, Shui Ta. Should Miss Shen Te really come back, the young man's presence would be highly improper. As we know, he once exerted a most harmful influence over her.

SHUI TA (*bowing*): Doubtless. Please excuse my long hesitation over the question of my cousin Shen Te and Mr. Yang Sun. It is not worthy of a businessman. But they were once very close to each other.

THE LANDLADY: You're excused.

SHUI TA (*looking toward the door*): My friends, let us now reach a settlement. In this once small and shabby store where the poor people of the neighbor hood bought the good Shen Te's tobacco, we, her friends, are resolving to establish twelve beautiful new stores which in the future will sell Shen Te's good tobacco. I'm told people are calling me the Tobacco King of Setzuan. Actually I carried on this business solely in my cousin's interests. It will belong to her, her children, and her grandchildren.

[*The noise of a crowd can be heard from outside. Enter Sun, Wang, and the Policeman.*]

THE POLICEMAN: Mr. Shui Ta, I'm very sorry the excited state of this neighborhood forces me to follow up a report originating in your own firm. According to this report you are depriving your cousin Miss Shen Te of her freedom.

SHUI TA: It's not true.

THE POLICEMAN: Mr. Yang Sun here testifies that from the room behind your office he heard sobbing which could only come from a female.

THE LANDLADY: That's ridiculous. I and Mr. Shu Fu, two respected citizens of this city whose evidence could hardly be doubted by the police, can testify that no one has been sobbing here. We are quietly smoking our cigars.

THE POLICEMAN: Unfortunately I have orders to inspect the room in question.

[*Shui Ta opens the door. The Policeman bows and steps into the doorway. He looks into the room, then turns round and smiles.*]

THE POLICEMAN: There's really nobody in there.

SUN (*who has been following him*)**:** But I heard sobbing! (*His eye lights on the table under which Shui Ta has pushed the bundle. He spots the bundle.*) That wasn't here before!

[*Opening it, he shows Shen Te's dresses and other things.*]

WANG: Those are Shen Te's things! (*He runs to the door and calls out.*) Her clothes have been discovered here!

THE POLICEMAN (*taking the things*)**:** You declare that your cousin's gone away. A bundle with things of hers is found hidden under your table. Where can the girl be reached, Mr. Shui Ta?

SHUI TA: I don't know her address.

THE POLICEMAN: That is most regrettable.

SHOUTS FROM THE CROWD: Shen Te's things have been found! The Tobacco King has murdered the girl and put her out of the way!

THE POLICEMAN: Mr. Shui Ta, I shall have to ask you to follow me to the station.

SHUI TA (*bowing to the Landlady and Mr. Shu Fu*): I have to apologize for this scandal, my friends. But there are still judges in Setzuan. I'm convinced that everything will shortly be cleared up. (*He goes out, the Policeman at his back.*)

WANG: A terrible crime has been committed!

SUN (*dismayed*): But I heard sobbing!

ACT 9-A

[*Wang's sleeping quarters. Music. For the last time the Gods appear to the water seller in his dream. They have changed considerably. There are unmistakable signs of a long journey, extreme exhaustion, and manifold unhappy experiences. One has had his hat struck off his head, one has lost a leg in a fox trap, and all three go barefoot.*]

WANG: At last you've come! Terrible things have been happening in Shen Te's tobacco store, illustrious ones. Shen Te went away again many months ago! Her cousin seized everything! Today he's been arrested. He's supposed to have murdered her to get her store. But I don't believe it. I had a dream in which she came and told me that her cousin's holding her prisoner. Oh, illustrious ones, you must come back at once and find her.

THE FIRST GOD: This is terrible. Our whole search has come to grief. We didn't find many good people and those we found lived in a way quite unworthy of human beings. We'd already decided to confine ourselves to Shen Te.

THE SECOND GOD: If she's still good!

WANG: She certainly is, but she's disappeared!

THE FIRST GOD: Then all is lost.

THE SECOND GOD: Restrain yourself!

THE FIRST GOD: What good would that do? If she can't be found, we've got to retire. What sort of world did we find? Misery, vulgarity, and waste everywhere! Even the countryside has fallen away from us. The lovely trees are decapitated by telephone wires and on the other side of the mountains we see heavy smoke clouds and hear the thunder of cannon. And nowhere a good man who can pull through!

THE THIRD GOD: Alas, water seller, our commandments seem to be deadly. I fear that all our moral rules have to be done away with. People keep busy just saving their skins. Good intentions bring them to the brink of the abyss, and good deeds throw them into it. (*To the other two Gods*) The world can't be lived in, you've got to admit!

THE SECOND GOD (*vehemently*)**:** No, it's people who are worthless!

THE THIRD GOD: The world is too cold!

THE SECOND GOD: People are too weak!

THE FIRST GOD: Dignity, my friends, dignity! Brothers, we mustn't despair. We did find one human being who was good and stayed good. She's only disappeared. Let's hurry and find her! One is enough! Didn't we say that everything can still turn out well if there's one human being who can stand this world? Just one?

[*They quickly disappear.*]

ACT 10

[A courtroom. Groups: Mr. Shu Fu and the Landlady. Sun and his mother. Wang, the Carpenter, the Grandfather, the young Prostitute, the Old Man and Woman. Mrs. Shin, the Policeman. The Unemployed, the Sister-in-law.]

THE OLD MAN: He's too powerful.

WANG: He wants to open twelve new stores.

THE CARPENTER: How can the judge give a fair sentence if the accused's friends—the barber Shu Fu and the landlady Mi Tzu—are also his friends?

THE SISTER-IN-LAW: Mrs. Shin was seen last night carrying a fat goose into the judge's kitchen by order of Mr. Shui Ta. The fat was dripping through the basket.

THE OLD WOMAN (*to Wang*)**:** Our poor Shen Te will never be found.

WANG: No, only the gods can discover the truth.

THE POLICEMAN: Order! The judges are coming!

[Enter the three Gods in judges' robes. As they walk by the footlights on their way to their seats, one can hear them whispering.]

THE THIRD GOD: We'll be found out. The certificates are very badly forged.

THE SECOND GOD: And people will wonder about the judge's sudden indigestion.

THE FIRST GOD: No, that's only natural. He ate half a goose.

MRS. SHIN: These are new judges!

WANG: And very good ones!

[*The third and last God hears this, turns round, and smiles at Wang. The Gods sit down. The First God beats on the table with a hammer. The Policeman brings in Shui Ta who is whistled at but walks with lordly steps.*]

THE POLICEMAN: Be prepared for a surprise. It isn't the just Fu Yi Tcheng. But the new judges look very mild too.

[*Shui Ta sees the Gods and faints.*]

THE YOUNG PROSTITUTE: What's the matter? The Tobacco King has fainted.

THE SISTER-IN-LAW: Yes, at the sight of the new judges!

WANG: He seems to know them! I don't understand that.

THE FIRST GOD: Are you the tobacco merchant Shui Ta?

SHUI TA (*weakly*)**:** Yes.

THE FIRST GOD: You have been accused of doing away with your own cousin Miss Shen Te, in order to take possession of her business. Do you plead guilty?

SHUI TA: No.

THE FIRST GOD (*turning the pages of documents*)**:** We'll first hear the policeman of this neighborhood on the reputation of the accused and on the reputation of his cousin.

THE POLICEMAN (*stepping forward*)**:** Miss Shen Te was a girl who liked to please everyone, who lived and let live, as the saying goes. Mr. Shui Ta, on the other hand, is a man of principle. The generosity of Miss Shen Te forced him at times to strict measures. However, unlike the girl, he was always on the side of the law, your honor. Once, people to whom his cousin trustfully gave shelter were unmasked by him as a band of thieves. Another time he saved Miss Shen Te at the last moment from plain perjury. I know Mr. Shui Ta to be a respectable and law-abiding citizen.

THE FIRST GOD: Are there others present who want to testify that the accused is incapable of his supposed crime?

[*Mr. Shu Fu and the Landlady step forward.*]

THE POLICEMAN (*whispering to the Gods*)**:** Mr. Shu Fu, a very influential gentleman.

MR. SHU FU: Mr. Shui Ta has the reputation of a highly respected businessman here in Setzuan. He is Vice-President of the Chamber of Commerce and is about to be made justice of the peace.

WANG (*interrupting*)**:** By you! You're doing business with him!

THE POLICEMAN (*whispering*)**:** A disagreeable character.

THE LANDLADY: As President of the Community Chest I'd like to call the attention of the court to this fact: Mr. Shui Ta is not only about to give to his numerous employees the best possible rooms, well-lighted and healthy, but is also making regular contributions to our home for the disabled.

THE POLICEMAN (*whispering*)**:** Mrs. Mi Tzu, a close friend of the judge Fu Yi Tcheng!

THE FIRST GOD: Yes, yes, but now we've got to hear whether anyone has less favorable evidence to bring forward.

[*Wang, the Carpenter, the Old Man and Woman, the Unemployed, the Sister-in-law and the Young Prostitute step forward.*]

THE POLICEMAN: The scum of the neighborhood.

THE FIRST GOD: Well, what do you know of the general behavior of Shui Ta?

SHOUTS (*jumbled*)**:** He's ruined us!

—He blackmailed me!

—He led us off on the wrong track!

—Exploited the helpless!

—Lied!

—Cheated!

—Murdered!

THE FIRST GOD: Accused, what have you to say?

SHUI TA: I have simply enabled my cousin to exist, your honor. I only came when she was in danger of losing her little store. I had to come three times. I never wanted to stay. But the last time circumstances forced me to remain. I never had anything but trouble. My cousin was popular; I did the dirty work. That's why I'm hated.

THE SISTER-IN-LAW: You certainly are. Take our case, your honor! (*To Shui Ta*) I won't mention the sacks.

SHUI TA: Why not? Why not?

THE SISTER-IN-LAW (*to the Gods*)**:** Shen Te gave us shelter and he had us arrested.

SHUI TA: You stole cakes!

THE SISTER-IN-LAW: Now he pretends to be interested in the baker's cakes! He wanted the store for himself!

SHUI TA: The store wasn't a public refuge, selfish creatures!

THE SISTER-IN-LAW: But we had no place to stay!

SHUI TA: There were too many of you!

WANG: And they (*pointing to the Old Man and Woman*) were selfish too?

THE OLD MAN: We put our savings into Shen Te's store. Why did you make us lose our store?

SHUI TA: Because my cousin was helping a flier to fly. I was to get the money!

WANG: Maybe she wanted to help him to fly. What interested you was the well-paid job in Peking. The store wasn't good enough for you!

SHUI TA: The rent was too high!

MRS. SHIN: That's true enough.

SHUI TA: And my cousin knew nothing about business!

MRS. SHIN: That's true too! She was also in love with the flier.

SHUI TA: Shouldn't she be allowed to love?

WANG: Certainly! And why did you want to force her to marry a man she did not love, the barber over there?

SHUI TA: The man she loved was a scoundrel.

WANG (*pointing to Sun*)**:** Him?

SUN (*jumping up*)**:** And because he was a scoundrel you took him into your office!

SHUI TA: To improve you! To improve you!

THE SISTER-IN-LAW: To make him into a slave-driver!

WANG: And when he was improved, didn't you sell him to her? (*Pointing to the Landlady*) She shouted it around every place!

SHUI TA: Because she wouldn't give me her buildings unless she had him to stroke her knees!

THE LANDLADY: That's a lie! Don't talk of my buildings ever again. I'll have nothing more to do with you. Murderer! (*She rustles off, insulted.*)

SUN (*insisting on getting his word in*)**:** Your honor, I must speak on his behalf!

THE SISTER-IN-LAW: Naturally. You're in his employ.

THE UNEMPLOYED: He's the worst slave-driver I've ever known. He's absolutely depraved.

SUN: Your honor, the accused may have made whatever you say of me, but he's not a murderer. A few minutes before he was arrested I heard Shen Te's voice in his back room!

THE FIRST GOD (*avidly*)**:** So she's alive? Tell us exactly what you heard? SUN (*triumphantly*): Sobbing, your honor, sobbing!

THE THIRD GOD: And you recognized her?

SUN: Absolutely. How could I fail to recognize her voice?

MR. SHU FU: Sure, you made her sob often enough!

SUN: And yet I made her happy. But then he (*pointing to Shui Ta*) wanted to sell her to you!

SHUI TA (*to Sun*)**:** Because you didn't love her!

WANG: No. For the money!

SHUI TA: But what was the money needed for, your honor? (*To Sun*) You wanted her to sacrifice all her friends, but the barber offered his cabins and his money to help the poor. Moreover, I had to get her engaged to him so that she could still be good.

WANG: Why didn't you let her be good when the big check was signed? Why did you send Shen Te's friends into the dirty sweatshops of your factory, To bacco King?

SHUI TA: For the child's sake!

THE CARPENTER: And my children? What did you do with my children?

[*Shui Ta is silent.*]

WANG: Now you're silent! The gods gave the store to Shen Te as a little fountain of goodness. She always wanted to do good and you always came and spoiled it.

SHUI TA (*beside himself*)**:** Because otherwise the fountain would have dried up, fool!

MRS. SHIN: That's true, your honor!

WANG: What good is a fountain if you can't get at the water?

SHUI TA: Good deeds mean ruin!

WANG (*wildly*)**:** But bad deeds mean a good life, don't they? What did you do with the good Shen Te, bad man? How many good people are there, illustrious ones? She was good! When that man over there smashed my hand, she wanted to testify for me. And now I testify for her. She was good, I swear! (*He raises his hand in an oath.*)

THE THIRD GOD: What's the matter with your hand, water seller? It's all stiff.

WANG (*pointing to Shui Ta*)**:** It's his fault, his alone! She wanted to give me money for the doctor but then he came along! You were her deadly enemy!

SHUI TA: I was her only friend!

ALL: Where is she?

SHUI TA: Gone away!

WANG: Where to?

SHUI TA: I won't tell!

ALL: And why did she have to go away?

SHUI TA (*shouting*)**:** Because you would have tom her to shreds! (*Sudden quiet. He sinks onto a chair*) I can't go on. I'll explain everything. If the hall is cleared and only the judges remain, I will make a confession.

ALL: He's confessing! He's found out!

THE FIRST GOD (*beating on the table with the hammer*)**:** Let the hall be cleared!

[*The Policeman clears the hall.*]

MRS. SHIN (*laughing as she goes*)**:** There'll be a surprise!

SHUI TA: Have they gone? All of them? I can no longer keep silence. I recognized you, illustrious ones!

THE SECOND GOD: What did you do with our good woman of Setzuan?

SHUI TA: Let me confess the terrible truth: I am she!

THE SECOND GOD: Shen Te!

SHEN TE:

Yes, it is I. Shui Ta and Shen Te. I am both.
Your former injunction to be good and yet to live
Tore me like lightning in halves.
I don't know how it happened.
To be good to others and to myself
I couldn't do both at the same time.
To help others and to help myself was too hard.
Alas, your world is difficult! Too much misery, too much despair!
The hand that is extended to a beggar, the beggar at once tears off!
Whoever helps the lost is lost himself!
For who could long refuse to be bad when he who eats no meat must die?

All the things that were needed where should I have taken them from?
From myself! But then I perished!
A load of good intentions weighed me down to the ground.
Yet when I was unjust I walked mightily about and ate good meat!
Something must be wrong with your world.
Why is malice well rewarded? Why do punishments await the good?
Oh, how I should have loved to pamper myself!
And there was also a secret knowledge in me.
My foster-mother washed me in water from the gutter:
That gave me a sharp eye.
Yet pity pained me so, I was an angry wolf at the sight of misery.
Then I felt how I was changing and kind words turned to ashes in my mouth.
And yet I wished to be an Angel to the Suburbs.
To give was a delight. A happy face, and I walked on clouds.
Condemn me: everything I did I did to help my neighbor,
To love my lover, and to save my little son from want.
For your great plans, O gods! I was too poor and small.

THE FIRST GOD (*with all signs of horror*)**:** Don't go on, unhappy woman! What should we think, we who are so happy to have found you again!

SHEN TE: But I've got to tell you that I am the bad man whose Crimes everyone was talking about!

THE FIRST GOD: The good woman whose good deeds everyone was talking about!

SHEN TE: The bad man too!

THE FIRST GOD: A misunderstanding! Several unfortunate occurrences! Some heartless neighbors! An excess of zeal!

THE SECOND GOD: But how is she to go on living?

THE FIRST GOD: She can do it. She's strong, well built. She can stand a lot.

THE SECOND GOD: But didn't you hear what she said?

THE FIRST GOD (*vehemently*): It was confused, very confused! And incredible, highly incredible! Should we admit our commandments to be deadly? Should we renounce our commandments? (*Sullenly*) Never! Should the world be changed? How? By whom? No! Everything is in order! (*He suddenly beats on the table with the hammer.*) And now ... (*He makes a sign and music is heard. Rosy light.*) let us return.

This little world has much engaged us.
Its joy and its sorrow have refreshed and pained us.
Up there, however, beyond the stars,
We shall gladly think of you, Shen Te, the good woman
Who bears witness to our spirit down below,
Who, in cold darkness, carries a little lamp!
Goodbye! Do it well!

[*He makes a sign and the ceiling opens. A pink cloud comes down. On it the Three Gods rise, very slowly.*]

SHEN TE: Oh, don't, illustrious ones! Don't go away! Don't leave me! How can I face the good old couple who've lost their store and the water seller with his stiff hand? And how can I defend myself from the barber whom I do not love and from Sun whom I do love? And I am with child. Soon there'll be a little son who'll want to eat. I can't stay here!

[*She turns with a haunted look toward the door which will let her tormentors in.*]

THE FIRST GOD: You can do it. Just be good and everything will turn out well!

[*Enter the witnesses. They look with surprise at the judges floating on their pink cloud.*]

WANG: Show respect! The gods have appeared among us! Three of the highest gods have come to Setzuan to find a good human being. They had found one already, but...

THE FIRST GOD: No "but"! Here she is!

ALL: Shen Te!

THE FIRST GOD: She has not perished. She was only hidden. She will stay with you. A good human being!

SHEN TE: But I need my cousin!

THE FIRST GOD: Not too often!

SHEN TE: At least once a week!

THE FIRST GOD: Once a month. That's enough!

SHEN TE: Oh, don't go away, illustrious ones! I haven't told you everything! I need you desperately!

[*The Gods sing.*]

THE TRIO OF THE VANISHING GODS ON THE CLOUD

We, alas, may never stay
More than a fleeting year
If you watch your treasure long
'Twill always disappear.
Down here the golden light of truth
With shadow is alloyed
That is why we take our leave
And go back to our void.

SHEN TE: Help! (*Her cries continue through the song.*)
Our anxious search is over now
Let us to heaven ascend
The good, good woman of Setzuan

Praising, praising to the end!

[*As Shen Te stretches out her arms to them in desperation, they disappear above, smiling and waving.*]

EPILOGUE

[*One of the actors walks out in front of the curtain and apologetically addresses the audience.*]

Ladies and gentlemen, don't be angry! Please!
We know the play is still in need of mending.
A golden legend floated on the breeze, The breeze dropped, and we got a bitter ending.
Being dependent on your approbation
We wished, alas! our work might be commended.
We're disappointed too. With consternation
We see the curtain closed, the plot unended.
In your opinion, then, what's to be done?
Change human nature or—the world? Well: which?
Believe in bigger, better gods or—none?
How can we mortals be both good and rich?
The right way out of the calamity
You must find for yourselves. Ponder, my friends,
How man with man may live in amity
And good men—women also—reach good ends.
There must, there must, be some end that would fit.
Ladies and gentlemen, help us look for it!

— END —